OUR AMERICAN JOURNEY

A History of the Brighton Nisei Women's Club and the
Brighton Japanese American Association

Daniel Blegen

outskirtspress

DENVER, COLORADO

*Dedicated to the Issei and Nisei
without whom the journey would
not have been possible.*

Table of Contents

Preface

The prospect of turning nine years old fires up most third graders with pleas for presents. They write urgent requests in lengthy birthday lists on notebook paper in a penciled scrawl and exploratory spellings. Their desires are stoked by toy companies hawking the latest, hottest, just-gotta-have gimmicks that assault target audiences – kids and parents alike – on TV ads during children's programming. As any parent knows, many of those gotta-have gifts gather dust under bunk beds, sometimes before the helium has leaked from the party balloons.

But one Brighton eight-year-old wanted just a single gift for her ninth birthday. It had not been advertised on television. It could not have been described by the words "latest" or "hottest." Nor would Lindsay Kline abandon it once her special day had passed. She would keep and cherish this gift for the rest of her life: Lindsay wanted a new middle name.

She wasn't dissatisfied with the middle name her parents had given her at birth. She wasn't embarrassed by it or ashamed of it. "Marie" was easy to spell, even for a third grader. It just didn't announce the strong connection she was feeling to her mom's Japanese heritage, a heritage she had found nestled in the arms of her grandfather, Sumiji Horii. Horii had celebrated his first sixteen birthdays in Japan, before immigrating to Colorado by way of California. Here, he nurtured in his granddaughter a wonder for roots, for faraway places, and an entirely different culture both new and ancient to the eyes and ears of an American girl.

On her ninth birthday, Lindsay Kline, daughter of Tom and Linda Kline, got her birthday wish. Lindsay Marie became Lindsay Sumiko Kline - Sumiko being the feminine form of Sumiji. In court, that formal change merely made official what had been a reality in her heart. Now a married woman, Lindsay Sumiko (Kline) Auker recently completed a degree at the University of Northern Colorado in education. She is an active member of the Brighton Japanese American Association (BJAA). Her story echoes one of the initial impulses prompting the formation of the Brighton Nisei Women's Club (BNWC) and the BJAA: the impulse to preserve one's ethnic heritage.

Emi Chikuma made it her personal mission to do just that for over eighty years. She was well-versed in the extended Japanese family in the Brighton, Colorado, area. Her immigrant parents – Tanemi and Miyo Katagiri – owned a general store south of town where she heard *Issei* farmers and their picture-bride wives reminiscence about a homeland so foreign from her own. At Hazeltine Elementary School, Chikuma learned English and, with her classmates, melded into a unique generation that would prove itself worthy of its American citizenship, despite the injustices that would be thrown their way. As a teenager, she drove to the wholesale markets in Denver, picking up stock for the family's store and expanding her acquaintance with the broad swath of the Issei and *Nisei* experience. As an adult, of course, she joined the Brighton Nisei Women's Club, though official membership was just a formality for one already so much a part of the community. Chikuma took her turn as president of the BNWC, but a role she continued to fill was "Unofficial BNWC/BJAA Historian."

With Chikuma, all conversational roads led back to sports: BJAA softball, baseball, basketball as well as bowling, golf and judo. They are the pantheon of BJAA's active past. Sports coached by the men of the Nisei generation; played by their kids. Sports kept those kids exercised, connected, and out of trouble. Softball in Brighton even enabled a young woman named Nancy Ito to shine all the way to induction in the National Softball Hall of Fame in 1982. Year after year, as early as the 1920s, those young, amateur athletes posed for team pictures. In the photos they beam with accomplishment, pride of ownership, and belonging. For two or three generations of young men, BJAA-sponsored sports defined lives and directed futures.

Emi Chikuma had long been wise to the need for preservation. She was a walking storehouse of knowledge of the BJAA and the broader experience of Japanese Americans in Colorado. "I got stuff," she once said. "I got stuff, you don't know." Then in a tone of voice suggesting the visitor to her home not argue the point, she repeated for emphasis, "I got stuff." In addition to her vivid memories, that "stuff" was the stuff of an historian's dreams: photos, newspaper articles, programs – printed memorabilia from six decades of clipping and saving. All of it organized chronologically, eventful year by eventful year, in scrapbooks that lined sagging shelves in Chikuma's basement, scrapbooks as large as tax rolls or the quartos of a hermit monk bent on preserving a way of life that was rapidly disappearing. And lists of names, the names of the children of Adams and Weld County Japanese American families, in descending order of age, with only periodic gaps where the name of a sibling here or there had been temporarily lost to memory. She was stumped at times, but the lost name would eventually come to her or be sought from friends, often with a softball statistic attached or the exact location of a family farm house long fallen to the winds of change.

On top of a ping pong table in her basement, Chikuma often laid out those portfolios for an interested writer – in an order that made perfect sense, if only to her. On the table, faces from overlapping generations mingled like long-lost friends or relatives at a family reunion. In effect, that's what they were.

The Issei generation, which began arriving in Colorado in the late nineteenth century, was isolated from the larger community by a language barrier. Social isolation prompted their Nisei daughters to organize the BNWC in 1948. Two years later, the Nisei men also organized, although their intents were many-fold and somewhat paradoxical. They too felt a need for socialization, but in post-World War II Brighton their overriding desire was to counteract the bitter discrimination that lingered in the wake of Japan's devastating war against the U.S. With the BJAA, the Nisei men hoped to spotlight their loyalty to America, the country to which they belonged and for which many had put their lives on the line during the war. They would prove their loyalty again in action, reaching out in service to the Brighton community. The parallel purposes of socialization, cultural preservation and community service continue.

A successful organization is not an inanimate object. It is the combined force of individuals promoting common causes. In part it is the sum of the life stories lived by those individuals. So, this history of the Brighton Nisei Women's Club and the Brighton Japanese American Association is really a group biography of the individuals and families who founded and sustained the formal organizations. That biography begins with the Issei (pronounced ē′ sā) who settled into the Platte Valley as early as 1900. From their first, tenuous attempts at farming grew an admirable stability. Their stories, however, are not widely known, even within Colorado. An informal survey of their great grandchildren, now college age, indicates that the younger generation knows very little about their ancestors' early accomplishments or the needs that prompted the formation of the two Nisei (nē′ sā) organizations some sixty years ago.

In recent years, the loss of Issei and Nisei leaders in the area's Japanese American community – including Emi Chikuma who passed away in March 2013 – called attention to the need for a formal telling of their story. That was the goal of the BJAA history committee in commissioning this book. Hopefully, that goal has been met, at least in part. Emi Chikuma's memories and her collection of primary resources made it possible, as did the comments shared by many other organization members. Without her and the others, this history would not have come to fruition.

CHAPTER ONE:

The Immigrants

As the nineteenth century drew to a close, families in Japan were looking into the face of the future. It stared back at them with hungry eyes indicative of an empty belly. Their numbers were slowly but steadily expanding; their homeland's boundaries – and its arable land – were not. The dilemma started literally at the water's edge, where the Sea of Japan to the west and the Pacific Ocean to the east precluded any prospect of expansion in farm production for the island nation.

A growing population might have signaled promise for the country's farm sector. It did not. Despite the ingenuity the farmers of Japan had inherited from their forefathers, who had long coaxed maximum harvests from minimal acreage, they foresaw only a future of diminishing returns. Inventiveness and the willingness to work could no longer support Japan's growing farm workforce. And despite the official demise of a centuries-old class system, under which farmers had been given higher status than shopkeepers, the opportunities for upward mobility remained as severely limited in agriculture as it was in other fields. Japan's farmers clearly saw the dilemma.

Their sons – by the thousands – looked for ways to escape it. That meant leaving Japan. The young men on Japan's farms were not the first group in the century with reason to leave their homes. Famine in the 1840s had pushed the Irish in desperate numbers from their own island nation. During the years leading up to 1900, millions of other Europeans also sensed the specter of want, or its discouraging cousin: hopelessness.

The decision to leave Japan may have been prompted by a set of factors more complex than basic economic need. The stories of a few of the young Japanese men who settled along the Platte Valley in Colorado between 1900 and 1910 shed light on that complexity. Their experiences also inform the eventual formation of the BNWC and BJAA. Kotaro Ida was one of them. He made the bold decision to leave his parents' farm and Japan to build a life from scratch in America. The opinion is still held within his family that Ida's decision may in fact have been bittersweet. He may have wanted to stay and take over the family farm, but according to his grandson, Ron Ida of Brighton, "In Japan, the oldest got everything, even if he was a bad guy or a crook." Kotaro was the Idas' second son, and therefore prohibited by Japanese tradition from inheriting the family land. The tradition's mandate was firm, according to Ida. And the scarcity of arable land in Japan eliminated the possibility of buying other acreage. Ron Ida recalled his Japanese American friends telling similar stories about their grandfathers, who were also younger siblings with no hope of inheriting land.

Other, young Japanese men were simply pushed out by bad luck. After serving with the Japanese army in China, Kaisaku Horiuchi began raising silk worms. The business profited until a flood destroyed his entire operation. He started a charcoal manufacturing plant, but it burned down. Then he found work on an ocean-going vessel. The sea was evidently not for him. He jumped ship in New York. Horiuchi worked his way across America to Washington state, where he worked in a saw mill. When he was financially stable, he leased a farm and sent for his wife and children. Eventually they found their way to Colorado, where Horiuchi's two brothers joined him. Some sources say that in the early 1900s there was a nationwide "emigration fever" among Japan's young men, stoked by the publication of more than ten different how-to manuals on the ins and outs of establishing a new life abroad.

Another harsh reality in Japan prompted others to leave: the threat of war. In 1894 Japan had defeated China in the Sino-Japanese War. Those in power in Japan wanted to enlarge their country's presence and influence in the Chinese territories they had seized. This lead to friction with Russia, which was eyeing the same areas. In 1903, with the obvious approach of war between the two emerging empires, many young men balked at the notion of being drafted into the Japanese military for yet another foreign war. Some, such as attorney and judge Bunji Tokunaga, fled the country, fearing that his political opinions might result in government persecution. Indeed, a war, now known as the Russo-Japanese War, broke out the next year.

Magosaburo Tanaka, from Nagano in Japan's lake country northwest of Tokyo, stayed and served in the war before immigrating to Colorado. He encouraged his brother Junzo to follow him and avoid being drafted into combat. Junzo took his brother's advice and joined him in Pueblo, Colorado, in 1907 when he was just eighteen. Junzo set his sights on enrollment at the University of Denver and worked in Pueblo's steel mills to raise tuition money. Instead, his path led him into farming in northern Colorado, in Hazeltine south of Brighton, where he lived for more than fifty years.

Another factor that might have drawn Japan's young men to the United States was - quite ironically - racism. In the mid-1800s, Chinese immigrants had found jobs in the American West, laying tracks for the Union Pacific Railroad and later digging coal from mines owned by the same company. They also found discrimination. Their insular nature and carefully preserved cultural identity were perceived by Whites as suspect and prompted malicious rumors. The Chinese became the target of violence in many cities in the West, some of the worst incidents in Los Angeles in 1870 and San Francisco in 1877. In Denver in 1880, a mob of rioters destroyed all of the homes and businesses owned by the Chinese residents of the city.

Anti-Chinese sentiments reached all the way to Washington, D.C. In 1882, Congress passed the Chinese Exclusion Act, which prohibited any more Chinese from immigrating into the country for ten years. Using a now-familiar argument, the proponents of the act argued that the Chinese were taking jobs from White Americans by working for lower wages. The Chinese Exclusion Act did little to end the racism, or the violence, aimed at those already in the United States. In September 1885, following an ongoing labor dispute over Union Pacific's policy of hiring Chinese coal miners at wages lower than those demanded by White miners, large-scale rioting erupted in Rock Springs, Wyoming Territory. Rioters burned seventy-five Chinese homes. They killed twenty-eight Chinese miners and injured fifteen more.

Into this racially charged environment just fifteen years later stepped the young Japanese emigrants. In Colorado, Wyoming, and other mountain states, they took up the jobs forcibly vacated by the Chinese, providing the same so-called "cheap source of labor" desired by corporate owners. Yet somehow the Japanese fared better – much better – than their Asian neighbors who had come before them. At least in the early years of the twentieth century. According to statistics recorded by researchers at the University of California, in 1900 the number of Japanese across America was 24,000. By 1910, that number had tripled to 72,000. U.S. Census records show the same population trend occurred within Colorado. In 1900, only fifty-one Japanese residents were counted in the state. By 1910, the number had risen to an estimated twenty-three hundred. Of the several reasons for the increase, one was certainly the violent boycott that had purged the Chinese from the American work force in the West.

Whether or not the violence directed at the Chinese immigrants was widely known in Japan, it is obvious that the Japanese truly believed that a better future could be created in a country such as the United States. In a mirror image of the massive exodus of Europeans taking place at the time, the sons of Japan booked passage on steam ships plying east across the Pacific. Some disembarked in Hawaii, where they found work on farm plantations. Some sailed on to Canada and the countries of South America. Most headed for the U.S. The Japanese emigrated in smaller numbers than the Norwegians or Germans or Greeks, but they left their homes with the same hopes. Unlike the sons of Europe - who more often than not emigrated with their wives, parents, and siblings - the sons of Japan traveled alone or in small groups from the same village. Most crossed the Pacific - figuratively, if not literally - in the same boat. A few were already married but left their wives and children behind, often working for years before financial stability enabled them to reunite their families. Most were single men. In fact, for a short time at the turn of the twentieth century, Japanese immigrants in the U.S. were a generation of bachelors.

For those who disembarked in Seattle, with Mount Rainier Fuji-like in the distance, the new home probably seemed little different from the old. Inland America, however, must have provided quite a contrast. One can only imagine the thoughts of a Japanese farm boy, accustomed to the narrow valleys and terraced hillsides of his small island, first encountering the prairies of Wyoming and Colorado, where horizons were as wide as those he had seen during his ocean passage. The U.S. had so much land; so much of it untouched by a plow. Colorado must have seemed like a farmer's nirvana - hot and dry in the summer to be sure, but nirvana nonetheless.

Once in America, Kotaro Ida, Kaisaku Horiuchi, and Magosaburo Tanaka took surprisingly similar, if meandering, paths. They crossed the docks of California and Washington, climbed the Rockies, and embraced the Great Plains, where other young men from Japan were settling along the South Platte River between Denver and the Wyoming state line and east to Nebraska. Years later, the names of their sons and daughters – and those of many other Japanese immigrants – would be found in the membership rolls of the BNWC and the BJAA.

Gohachi Nakata was one of the first Japanese emigrants who found a new home along the South Platte River. His story bears witness to his determination and that of the others in his generation. In a country such as Japan, where one's ancestry was ancient and grandparents and parents were venerated, the obligation to stay would have been strong, an ancestral inertia. Then again, staying might have meant becoming the final member of an ancient family driven to the edge of starvation. Not an attractive option. So as the past urged Nakata to stay, the future beckoned. Even with its unknown challenges, the future won the inner conflict. He would reimagine his future in a new century in a new country. That reimagining included a definite sense of permanence. Gohachi Nakata – as well as the other young men in his situation – saw himself as part of the first of many generations in America. Even the label that he and the others used to identify themselves declared that sense of permanence. They would be the Issei: the first generation.

A married man, Gohachi Nakata still worked with his parents in Kumamoto on the southern island of Kyushu. They grew rice, wheat, and millet on just three acres of farm land. He had married Toku Noguchi, and they had two sons, Takeshi (Frank) and Tadashi (James). From family and friends, Nakata repeatedly heard the conventional wisdom of the day: "If you go to America, you will get rich." An overstatement, certainly, and yet there was evidence to support that mantra.

Indeed, during the 1870s and 1880s the American economy had grown at the fastest rate in its history, prompting novelist Mark Twain to label the period the Gilded Age. The waves of European immigrants who were rapidly expanding the population were providing not only the laborers to increase the country's farm production and industrial output but also the consumers to buy its products. Between 1865 and 1898, U.S. wheat production increased by 256 percent; corn production increased by 222 percent. The rail lines built during the same period extended the country's existing tracks by a whopping 567 percent. Over those rails would move the staples of industrial growth: coal and steel.

Between 1902 and 1908, the Japanese immigrants would pick up the railroad jobs that the Chinese had filled earlier. Preparing road beds and laying track was backbreaking work, but it provided an income for the immigrants. And mile by mile, railroad work showed them the lay of their new land. In Colorado, judging from where they ultimately settled, the sons of Japan's farmers found land with tremendous potential for farming along the South Platte River, in the St. Vrain Valley, and along the Arkansas River to the south.

When America beckoned Gohachi Nakata, he followed. His story begins, as many of the Issei immigration stories do, with these words: "He finally saved enough money to buy passage on a ship." But his money took him only as far as Hawaii, and so Hawaii became a working layover, as it would for other Issei. There, Nakata worked in the sugar cane fields until again "he saved enough money for passage to America." He landed in San Francisco in 1903. From California, Nakata moved inland. He found work laying railroad tracks in Wyoming and Colorado and clearing land for electric power lines to be strung between Denver and Boulder. Meanwhile, wife Toku, with the couple's two sons, ages five and three, continued to work the Nakata farm in Japan. She would not see her husband again for fourteen years.

Also arriving in 1903 was Magoki Masunaga, whose story resembles Nakata's. Masunaga too was a married man when he left Japan to pursue greater economic opportunity in the U.S. He too left his wife behind. Taki was pregnant with the

Masunagas' first child, a girl to be named Yoshiye. Masunaga would not be able to bring Taki to the U.S. for ten years. Even then the family decided that daughter Yoshiye should remain in Japan with her grandparents until completing her education. Magoki and Taki Masunaga farmed near Fort Lupton, and they had four other children. The first, born in 1914, was Yoshito – George – who as an adult would serve as the founding president of the BJAA. George was followed by brothers Jess and John and sister Mary. (According to Gordon Studebaker, a nephew by marriage, George did not meet his sister Yoshiye until 1934 when he accompanied his mom on a trip to Japan. The other U.S. siblings did not meet Yoshiye until 1960, when she was fifty-seven years old.)

Another farm boy from Fukuoka on the island of Kyushu was Katsubei Sakaguchi. He was a first-born son; yet even he wanted to leave the poverty of the family's rice farm. "Neither he nor his father had ever been outside his area in Japan," said Bob Sakaguchi, one of his grandsons. But they had heard that the sugar cane plantations in Hawaii were hiring field workers. The story circulating in Japan was that plantation owners were looking for workers willing to sign three-year work contracts. By the end of three years, the owners promised, a field hand could save $900 toward his future. That was a tempting sum of money. Sakaguchi implored his father for permission to sign a contract with the Kealia Sugar Plantation on the island of Kauai in Hawaii. His father finally relented. "Okay. Fine. I'll let you do that," he said. Sakaguchi left home in 1905, just twenty years old.

When he got to Hawaii, Sakaguchi found out very quickly that there was no way that he could ever save $900 working on the plantation. The promising sum had been at best an over-statement, at worst an outright deception. Sakaguchi was hired by Kealia Sugar at seventy-five cents per day for a six day week. From each paycheck the company deducted a charge for his room and board on the plantation.

Sakaguchi's hopes for the future were crushed. He worked the fields for less than a year; then he fled the plantation. Running away was no doubt the impulsive act of a young man, a young man suddenly alone and unemployed on a small island in the middle of the Pacific Ocean. But that fact may have troubled him less than his conscience did. "In the back of his mind," Bob Sakaguchi said of his grandfather, "he knew that he couldn't return to Japan." In abandoning his job, he had done more harm than merely losing a meager income. In the Japanese tradition, he had broken a contract - gone back on his word - and, in so doing, brought dishonor to himself and his entire family.

Then Sakaguchi met a Japanese woman who operated a hotel on Kauai. She sympathized with his situation and helped him obtain passage to Honolulu on the island of Oahu. From there, with only twenty dollars in his pocket, he managed to reach the United States. He arrived on the *S.S. Manchuria,* which docked in San Francisco on February 21, 1906. Family tradition suggests that he may have been a stowaway. He was then twenty-one years old. Almost immediately he found work with the Union Pacific Railroad, a lucky turn of events but not uncommon. Journalist Bill Hosokawa quoted an anonymous Issei "reminiscing about the early days" in America: "There was plenty of work. Two days after I came to this country, I had a job on the railroad. I could have worked on the railroad as long as I wanted. But I wanted to learn something besides railroad work. I wanted to learn English." Coincidentally, two other future Brighton residents also arrived in the U.S. in 1906: Gotaro Chikuma and Masaki Tashiro. Like Sakaguchi, Tashiro had also worked in Hawaii on a pineapple plantation before making his way to Colorado.

A major point of reference in the stories of the Issei whose port of entry was San Francisco is the earthquake and subsequent fire that destroyed that city. Sakaguchi missed it by days. On April 18, 1906, when the quake struck, he was already laying rails in Wyoming. Later he worked on the construction of a rail line from Cheyenne to Denver. It would be the job that first brought him through Brighton. At some point - possibly after honorably fulfilling his contract with Union Pacific - Sakaguchi decided to return to Japan and began saving for the trip. His thriftiness, however, was known to his Issei co-workers, as was his generosity. Some, who were needier or less thrifty themselves, began asking him for loans, which he felt compelled to make. The borrowers, unfortunately, felt less compelled to repay their debts and sank Sakaguchi's plans for a voyage home.

The Issei who moved inland also found work in agriculture and, to a lesser extent, in steel mills and coal mines. There were really few other options open to them. As many as 500 Issei worked at Colorado Fuel and Iron Company's steel mill in Pueblo, Colorado, at the turn of the century. Those who worked the hottest jobs, at the blast furnaces, could earn $2.50 in a ten-hour day. Others found work digging coal beneath the small mining towns north of Denver, such as Erie, Frederick, and Lafayette. In the mines, they found themselves in the same labor hotbed that the Chinese had endured decades earlier. "[I] t seems likely that some Japanese, either through ignorance or simple acceptance of whatever their bosses told them, worked in the mines for less money than Caucasians," wrote Bill Hosokawa, in his book *Nisei: The Quiet Americans*. Other Japanese were among those employed as strikebreakers in a series of labor disputes that wracked the coal industry, including in the coal fields of southern Colorado at the time of the Ludlow Massacre, in 1914.

Farming held the greatest attraction. Among the Issei who first settled into farming along the South Platte River, a surprisingly large number were from the southern Japanese island of Kyushu. Mantaro Sakata left the farm village of Kurume on the island in 1902. In the U.S. he first farmed in the San Francisco Bay area until 1942, when he was interned by the U.S. government following the Japanese attack on Pearl Harbor. After the war, he and his sons, Harry and Bob, founded Sakata Farms in Brighton, now one of the largest produce farms in the state. Beginning early in their careers, Harry and Bob Sakata would take on leadership roles in the BJAA and other service organizations. The Kyushu-Brighton connection is so obvious that it begs certain questions. Were farm conditions on Kyushu worse than in other regions of Japan, prompting greater numbers to leave? Once in the U.S., did the Kyushu men make a conscious effort to gather in the Brighton area? Or was it just good soil and available water that brought them together here? Whatever the case, farming was certainly a common denominator among the Kyushu men. Farming had been their lives on the island; they made it their livelihood on the plains of Colorado.

Nagahiko Mizunaga left Kyushu in 1904 at age nineteen. Like others on the island, he saw that the small farm could not support the growing Mizunaga family. He had developed skills as a stone carver and mason that he hoped to incorporate into a new career in America. But, Vicky Mizunaga Namura wrote of her family's history, "Perhaps the most convincing factor in [his] decision to move to America was [that] many of his village neighbors were also emigrating from Japan." The number of Brighton-area families with roots in Kyushu certainly bears witness to that statement. Making the requisite stop in Hawaii, Mizunaga joined a cousin on Maui and worked for two years in a sugar cane factory before leaving for the mainland. He recalled few details of his voyage, having slept most of the time, but did remember difficulties communicating with emigrants from Hiroshima, who spoke with a dialect different from what he was used to in his village, less than 200 miles to the south.

When the Issei arrived on the West Coast, they were recruited by *keiyaku-nin,* labor contractors. Contractors transported recruits to work sites, negotiated working conditions with employers, and served as on-the-job foremen and translators. For their services, contractors charged each laborer a fee. Some fees were exorbitant. One contractor for the Northern Pacific Railroad took ten cents from each man's daily wage, which was only $1.10 to begin with. And a contractor's fee did not necessarily assure good working conditions in return. Many Issei endured hardships during their years with the railroad companies. They often became sick from overwork and malnutrition. At night, they slept in boxcars pulled along the day's stretch of new track. "Life was hard for the young, vigorous, unattached immigrants," wrote Bill Hosokawa, "but it was not always grim." Hosokawa described the lot of the Japanese laborer in the early 1900s this way:

> Despite legal and social discrimination, economic hardship, unfamiliarity with language and customs, and strong ties of kinship and sentiment that linked them with the homeland, most of the young Issei found life in America interesting and not entirely unpleasant. Although they were aliens, they found their labor had value.

That sense of value was cultivated by one contractor in particular, whose reputation and accomplishments stood above the rest. Naoichi Hokasono endeared himself to the Issei generation by facilitating employment opportunities in Colorado for thousands of them. In addition, the construction projects they completed under his supervision placed Hokasono in the ranks of Colorado "state builders." Naoichi Hokasono - Harry - was a fellow Issei. Like Nakata, Sakaguchi, Sakata, and Mizunaga, he was born on Kyushu, but he had arrived in San Francisco much earlier than they, in 1884. In California he studied English and garnered experience in a variety of businesses before coming to Colorado in the winter of 1898. He began his career as a labor contractor in 1903 when he brought about seventy Japanese laborers from Rock Springs, Wyoming, to tend twelve hundred acres of sugar beets in northern Colorado near Greeley. As a labor contractor, Hokasono "probably more than any other man, was responsible for bringing the Japanese to [the Brighton] area." Harry was also one of the first to predict a bright future for Colorado agriculture.

A handful of photos exist of Hokasono. They show him to be a short, slight man with a boyish face and always the whisper of a smile, much softer looking than his grim, determined associates, both Japanese and White, posing in formal rows at crucial business and community meetings. He appears to be anything but the "mover and shaker" that he was. Only his position betrays his influence: front row center in every photo.

He was by all accounts a one-man dynamo. Even a brief review of his business accomplishments is awe inspiring. His crews not only did farm labor but also built irrigation systems, laid rail lines, graded highway routes, and cleared right of ways for power lines. Most of the work was done manually and with the help of draft animals. At one time, he owned more than a thousand horses and mules, used to pull earth-moving scoops.

Hokasono's company took part in the construction of one of the most ambitious railroad projects of the era. Begun in 1902, it was called the Moffat Road, named after its financial backer, Denver banker David Moffat, who had made a fortune in the gold fields of Florence and Cripple Creek in Colorado's mountains. Moffat's unbelievably ambitious "road" – actually the Denver, Northwestern, and Pacific Railroad – would begin in Denver, climb the Continental Divide, and roll through the towns of Grand County. The coal fields of the Colorado Western Slope and points beyond would be the line's ultimate destination. The rails pushed up the mountains until they reached a high point where a train station was built. Named Corona, in reference to its position as the crown of the continent, the station would mark the highest point in the world with a standard gauge railroad. Winter trips from Denver to Grand County on the Moffat Road were perilous at best.

Having crossed the mountains, the rail line reached Granby and Hot Sulphur Springs in 1905 and Kremmling in 1906. In April of 1908, the local newspaper in the town of Yampa, the *Yampa Leader*, informed readers that a crew hired by "prominent Denver contractor" Harry Hokasono was poised to build a twenty-mile section of rail north from their town to Steamboat Springs. "Before the end of the present month," the paper added, "several hundred Japanese laborers will be at work in the vicinity of this town." Those laborers - condescingly referred to in the article as "little brown men" and "Japs" - would be making a series of cuts through high spots on the planned route and surfacing the rail bed. Track building below Yampa was already progressing at a rate of one mile per day. At some point in the Moffatt Road project, Katsubei Sakaguchi joined Hokasono's work crew. Photographs from 1909 identify him somewhere along the route, enjoying what appears to be a well-deserved day off, dressed in his Sunday best.

Japanese Americans, including Katsubei Sakaguchi, constructed the Moffatt Road, actually the Denver, Northwestern and Pacific Railroad, across the mountains west of Denver. The workers, pictured here in 1909, were supervised by contractor Harry Hokasono.

Katsubei Sakaguchi (center) relaxed with coworkers on a day off from work on the Moffatt Road construction in 1909.

Beginning in 1908, Hokasono hired men for the construction of the Barker Dam and Reservoir in Boulder Canyon, just south of Nederland. The dam would provide hydroelectric power for Colorado's thriving mining camps and the booming city of Denver. Six of his men at the site were killed by an explosion when they didn't recognize the warning "Look out!" yelled in English. Hokasono was not aloof from the hardships of the workers. Having studied toward the *Higashi Hongwanji* priesthood while a boy in Japan, he conducted graveside services for some of the men who died in accidents or from illness due to lack of proper medical care.

Also in 1908, a busy year for Hokasono, his employees strung power lines between Denver and Georgetown and dug irrigation ditches near Trinidad, Loveland, and Longmont. In the 1920s, his company provided 600 men for the construction of the Moffat Tunnel, which replaced part of the Denver, Northwestern, and Pacific Railroad line making the perilous climb over the Continental Divide.

Harry Hokasono possessed talents outside the scope of business, too. Savvy to the power of the press, he expressed his opinions in a Japanese language newspaper, *Shin Sekai*, the *New World*, published in San Francisco and later in the Denver *Shimpo*, which he published as president of his own printing company. (A writer for the *Brighton Blade*, in a 1915 article, felt it necessary to mention that Hokasono "spoke English well.")

How does his story relate to the history of the Brighton Japanese American Association? Due to the employment opportunities he created, a number of Issei made Colorado home; their descendants in the Brighton area would become BJAA members. But more importantly, he was a role model for his fellow Issei by demonstrating the power of civic involvement and collective action. He served as the fourth president of an organization called the Japanese Committee of Colorado, organized in either 1907 or 1908, to calm anti-Japanese sentiments percolating among members of local labor unions upset with growing unemployment in the state. To demonstrate their sympathy with the unemployed, the membership made contributions to social service organizations such as the Salvation Army, which helped to ease hostile feelings aimed at them. Contributing to worthy causes in the community would become a hallmark of the BNWC and BJAA.

In 1915, Harry Hokasono served as president of both the Japanese Committee of Colorado – by then renamed the *Santoh Nihonjin Kai*, meaning Japanese Association – and the

Japanese Business Men's Association. That year, in his role as president of the Japanese Association, he attended a joint meeting with members of the Brighton branch of the organization and the Brighton Chamber of Commerce. The group stood for a photograph in front of a Brighton hotel where the meeting and a banquet were held. Hokasono is front and center. The *Brighton Blade* of March 4, 1915 commented that Hokasono was "obliged to leave the banquet early to attend another meeting" in Loveland, where he was involved in construction of an electric plant, a testament to a heavy work load. Somehow in his short but busy life, Hokasono also found time for a family. He and his wife adopted and raised two nieces. Teruko graduated from Brighton High School in 1931, Chizuko in 1934.

Hokasono's story, however, has a sad ending. What proved to be his last project was in the Wind River Canyon of Wyoming for the Denver and Rio Grande Railroad. To maintain a steady supply line there, his men used 300 donkeys to haul supplies from Casper. But engineering problems got the better of him. He lost $300,000 on the project. He died at his Brighton home in September, 1927 at age fifty-four, a poor and broken man. The local Nihonjin Kai collected donations for a headstone placed on Hokasono's grave in the Riverside Cemetery in Denver.

When railroad construction jobs pulled out of Colorado, the Issei called on the skills they had learned as young men in Japan and made the transition into farming. Some were helped in the transition by fellow Issei who had already established profitable farms in the state. Early in the century, both the Takakis near Ione, between Fort Lupton and Platteville, and the Mayedas, near Longmont, hired former railroad workers as farm hands. The "first generation" meant to put down roots in Colorado, both figuratively and literally. They were not content to be migrant workers, even though some had harvested sugar beets in Colorado under contract with Harry Hokasono and others. The Issei had a reputation in Colorado as good farmers, but as resident aliens they were hindered by law in many states from owning land. To that end, they worked through a progression of rites of passage, with sharecropping being the first. Lacking land and start-up funds, a sharecropper, nevertheless, possessed the knowledge and muscle necessary for farming. His success was dependent on finding a landowner willing to make the initial investments in seed and supplies, to provide farm equipment, and to allow access to his property.

At harvest time, the sharecropper paid the landowner back with a share of the profits, if any. In a printed interview in 1981, Helen Okada said, "Generally we gave one quarter [of the profits] to the landlord, and we got to keep the rest. [But] Grandpa had to buy the seed and whatever else to grow the crops. That's why it wasn't quite a half-and-half [business arrangement]."

Sharecropping was common for White farmers too, especially during the Depression of the 1930s. Oklahoma songwriter Woody Guthrie bemoaned the often sad lot of the sharecropper in the lyrics of his song "I Ain't Got No Home":

Was afarmin' on the shares, and always I was poor.

My crops I laid into the banker's store.

My wife lay down and died upon the cabin floor,

And I ain't got no home in this world anymore.

Well, obviously not all sharecroppers had it *that* hard.

If and when a sharecropper saved enough money, he could progress to a second and potentially more financially beneficial stage: land lease. Under a land lease agreement, a farmer would simply rent land from a landowner at a fixed rate. The costs of seed and supplies were shifted onto the farmer's shoulders. But land lease dangled a tasty carrot: the possibility of keeping all of one's profits. Profits - again, if any - would be reinvested in the following year's planting. The ultimate goal for many farmers, of course, and the final rite of passage, was land ownership.

An immigrant from Germany, O.E. Frink, played a significant role in attracting Issei farmers to the Platte River Valley to raise vegetables. In 1904 or 1905, Frink opened the Silver State Canning and Produce Company in Brighton. He helped Issei farmers lease land and arrange credit to buy seed and equipment. He then bought their produce and processed it in his plant. One of Frink's products, not surprisingly, was German sauerkraut, made from the locally grown cabbage.

Gohachi Nakata was one of the earliest to lease farm land in the area, although it took him three years of saving to do so. The 160 acres he leased southwest of Platteville was quite a contrast to the three acres his parents were farming in Japan, and even a bit larger than the average American farm a few years earlier in 1900, which was 147 acres. He would lease the Platteville farm for seven years, raising cabbage and sugar beets.

The *Brighton Blade* reported that in 1906 there were about one hundred Japanese "working in the beet fields at Brighton and Ft. Lupton in May 1906, and more in the summer time."

These were probably contract workers, because the same article states that there were forty-five Japanese farming the same area in 1908, probably the number sharecropping or leasing land.

Year by year, the Issei bachelor farmers began to marry and raise families. And they participated visibly in community life. In a historical review in the *Brighton Blade*, Albin Wagner commented:

> These Japanese families provided the most interesting feature of Ft. Lupton's first Tomato Day in 1908 performing Japanese dances and demonstrations of the martial arts...So many Japanese settled in the area that Ft. Lupton came to be nicknamed Yamato Village.

Despite their common immigration experiences, the Issei farming near Brighton did not immediately gel into a cohesive unit. Their areas of origin in Japan - their kens or prefectures - still held sway in their lives. There were immigrants from "certain prefectures that got along," said Ron Ida, "and other prefectures that didn't get along. So here in Colorado they stuck together by prefectures." Bob Sakaguchi grew up with a similar impression. "For example," he said, "the Fukuoka people congregated, and the Kyoto people kind of stuck together." Because those from the same prefecture could trace each other's families back to common roots, sticking together here gave them a way to keep in touch with Japan. If one of them got a letter from home, it might contain news of interest to the others from the same region.

Once in business for themselves, the Issei farmers also caught the bug of American competition, causing further rifts among them. Competition for land, especially, prompted the founding of The Japanese Association of Brighton, Fort Lupton and Platteville in 1908. One of the association's goals was to prevent "mutual conflicts," a goal that was evidently achieved. Members agreed that none would pay more than eighteen dollars per acre in rent for beet land, an arrangement that seems to have served a dual purpose: 1) keeping members from falling into "bidding wars" over the most productive fields and 2) putting landowners on notice that they would not be taken advantage of with high rents. A second goal - to force higher pay for Issei still doing farm work for contractors - was not met. One source sites the association's wage demands on behalf of its fellow Issei with the Northern Colorado Contractors Union as the cause of the association's disbanding. If true, The Japanese Association of Brighton, Fort Lupton, and Platteville had at least begun to cultivate the spirit of cooperation among its members.

In 1909, the Issei farmers organized again as the Japanese Farmers Association of Colorado, founded at a meeting in the Brighton town hall. George Sakikawa managed this organization and served as its spokesman. (There were as many Issei and Nisei organizations formed in the first half of the twentieth century as there were causes; many took similar names. The local historical record is limited and confusing on the topic. Adding to the confusion is the inclination among the Issei and Nisei to hold simultaneous memberships in multiple organizations.) Five years later, in 1914, the Issei founded a Brighton branch of the Colorado Nihonjin Kai mentioned above, the group for which Harry Hokasono served as state-wide president. George Sakikawa served on this group's board as well, along with

Tomotaro Okamoto, K. Hatakeyama, and Iso-o (Frank) Tanaka. Tanaka would also take personal leadership in 1920 in founding an independent Brighton Nihonjin Kai - also known as the Brighton Japanese Association (BJA). Japanese Americans were excluded from participation in all other civic and social organizations in Brighton, and yet, as Bob Sakata noted, the Issei recognized a need for some form of local organization to sponsor social events for themselves and their families. The BJA would be described as the "parent body from which most community endeavors flowed" in the 1920s and 1930s.

Public service was becoming part of the Issei mindset. In the spring of 1918, while U.S. troops in Europe were still mired in the trench warfare of World War I, Tomotaro Okamoto took part in a local drive to sell war bonds. The *Brighton Blade* acknowledged the generosity of farmers in an article that manages to be both gracious and racist, and surprisingly critical of an unnamed, local White land owner, it can be assumed:

> W.E. Shull, Axtel Johnson and T. Okamoto collected $2,000 from the Japs in and near Brighton Tuesday. Not one man refused to buy a bond and often they were large ones...One Japanese farmer living near Henderson purchased a $400 bond while his wealthy landlord refused to buy a $50 one. The Japanese are to be complimented upon their loyalty and support.

Cabbage growers – both Issei and White – united as the Colorado Cabbage Exchange, a wholesale marketing operation headquartered in Brighton. But in 1925, Japanese members of the exchange became embroiled in a conflict with other growers over prices. Cabbage production in the area had reached a peak between 1917 and 1924, when thousands of carloads of cabbage were being shipped yearly from the exchange's warehouse along the rail siding parallel to Second Avenue in Brighton, later renamed Cabbage Avenue. Japanese members felt they were not being treated fairly and called for a public audit of the exchange's finances before they would "entrust a whole year's product" to the market. They refused to sell their produce for what they considered too low a price, even though they had entered into contracts. In turn, an exchange spokesman threatened – in colorful language – a "regular orgy of contempt of court suits and damage suits." The secretary of the exchange, F.I. Kaihara, and a number of other local Japanese farmers were arrested in the conflict. Regional differences among the Issei themselves began to vanish of necessity. Again, Bob Sakaguchi pointed out, "They all kind of came together" around a common set of values and the same sense of organization. If they had some initial trouble understanding each other's regional dialects, they nevertheless shared a common language. They simply could not communicate at all with America's English-speaking population. Katsubei Sakaguchi would undertake the difficult task of teaching himself to read and write English.

However, Bob Sakaguchi added, in and around Brighton in the 1890s and early 1900s "you had Italians, Germans, Hispanics, Swedes up in the Greeley area, and then you had the Japanese. Those ethnic groups [each] stuck together. It was 'a natural thing.' And they each spoke their own native tongues." It's a factor that Sakaguchi found intriguing about Brighton's history. "There was more ethnic diversity in the Brighton area than in other communities, such as North Platte, Nebraska, where my grandparents on my mother's side came from."

North of Brighton, near Platteville, Gohachi Nakata threw his energy into farming. Meanwhile, in Japan his sons grew into young men. Takeshi - five years old the last time his father saw him - completed seven years of elementary school and then set his sights on possibly the only career choice open to him other than farming. He took and passed the entrance exam for Kamoto Chugako, Japan's most prestigious military training school. The specter of poverty for Takeshi Nakata seems to have lifted during his teen years at the military school. In a short autobiography, written when he was eighty-three years old, he mentioned participating in what are now typical school activities. He played on the baseball and tennis teams, and he set a school record in a two-mile swimming event. Takeshi Nakata also achieved in the classroom, graduating number thirteen in his class of one hundred, in March, 1917. The top fifteen graduates in the class, including Takeshi, received invitations from the Japan Naval Academy in Hiroshima to take its entrance exam. But just as Takeshi was to enter the academy, his father abruptly summoned him, along with his brother and mother, to the Platteville farm. After fourteen years, Gohachi Nakata was able to reunite his family in Colorado. Takeshi, poised at the verge of an auspicious academy appointment, must have been crushed. At the very least, he felt caught in the middle of an emotional dilemma. Sixty years later he wrote only this comment about leaving Japan: "I came to America because my father called me."

Many of Takeshi Nakata's classmates at Kamoto Chugako entered the academy. After their basic training, some rose in the ranks of the Japanese Navy; some became admirals, possibly those who led attacks against U.S. forces during World War II. One can only wonder what role Takeshi Nakata might have played in the war had his father not brought him to Colorado in the spring of 1917.

The brothers and their mother landed in Seattle, only to have the family's separation prolonged for yet another month. Toku's immigration papers had mistakenly been sent to San Francisco, so she was detained by officials in Seattle. Her younger son, Tadashi, went immediately to Colorado. Takeshi stayed with their mother and accompanied her on the train to Colorado when the paperwork snafu was cleared up. During his years in Platteville, Gohachi Nakata had been dubbed George, an Anglicized version of his name, a practice that became universal among his generation and the next. His son Tadashi would become James; Takeshi would become Frank.

In Colorado, Frank Nakata, who had been on the verge of a naval career in Japan, was introduced instead to raising cabbage and sugar beets. On the day following Frank's arrival in Platteville, the brothers were awakened by their dad at five A.M. to start hoeing and thinning in the fields. They worked till sundown. Looking at the Rocky Mountains to the west at the end of the day, Frank thought about his classmates in Japan, who were entering the military academy while he was scratching in the dirt. His friends were "advancing into the world," he wrote, "and I had to be in America to do farm work." Frank had arrived at a busy time of year, and he and James were called upon to work hard and long in the fields. "It was a lonely summer for me," Frank wrote, adding that for the duration of that summer he had only a half-a-day off work on the Fourth of July and another half-day off for Platteville's annual farm celebration, Pickle Day.

During the next seven years, George and Toku Nakata would make little profit, although they did add to their family: daughter Sadako (Rosie), born in 1918, and son Kyoshi (Henry), in 1920. In January of 1924, they leased a different 160-acre tract closer to Brighton. "It was a winter with hardly any snow," Frank Nakata wrote, and he did a late "fall plow" to get a jump on the next growing season. "Probably because of the plowing I did...we had a bumper crop of sugar beets" the next fall, when they harvested an average of twenty-two tons per acre. "We were number two in tonnage in the state of Colorado that year. As a reward, I received a watch from the sugar factory." The effects of the fall plow were also noticed by the Nakata's neighbors. After that year, Frank noted, "Everybody started to do their fall plowing."

In 1929, the family advanced to farm ownership. They bought eighty acres – located south of Brighton near Henderson, two miles east of Colorado Highway 85 on 120th Avenue – from the Rice family. No longer a lonely teenager envious of schoolmates back in Japan, Frank Nakata farmed the family's Colorado fields for forty-seven years before retiring and buying a home on Thirteenth Avenue in Brighton.

By 1911, Katsubei Sakaguchi had left railroad work for farming, the work he had known in Japan. The prospects for success appeared bright. In 1913, he wrote a letter home to his father, enlisting his help in finding a wife. Though an American by every right but citizenship, Sakaguchi remained loyal to the customs of his homeland where arranged marriages were still common, even the rule. (When Brighton resident Hisa Horiuchi spoke about her parents' arranged marriage, she mentioned that her mother admitted she didn't like her husband at first, but after moving to the U.S., in the early 1920s, she grew to love and respect him.) Marrying a White woman from the States was out of the question for the Issei, and few, single Japanese women lived here at the time. So in the early 1900s, an Issei bachelor had two options: returning to Japan to marry or arranging a marriage with a Japanese woman by mail. The latter was accomplished by exchanging photos with a woman, often a stranger, suggested by village elders or relatives in Japan. For a decade or two, the phenomenon of the "picture bride" marriage held sway. It was how most of the Issei women came to America. Tomotaro Okamoto's wife is said to be one of the first in Brighton. She had a reputation as one of the most beautiful "picture brides" in the area.

Yet, despite the acceptance of tradition, not every picture bride was happy with her situation. Some Issei men in the U.S. reportedly misrepresented themselves by sending photos of different men – younger and better looking, one can assume – when writing to prospective brides. Some of the fiancées, upon meeting their deceiving grooms face to face, "refused to get off the boat," according to Helen Okada. One was so disappointed in her prospective mate she said she would "rather die at sea than be married to the man who claimed to be her husband."

Returning to Japan to court a bride was impractical, though not unheard of. Masaki Tashiro was one of the few Colorado men who made the return trip. There he found Mata, only seventeen years old, and twenty years younger than he. Back in Brighton, Masaki, reportedly, had to teach Mata how to cook rice; other Issei wives taught her how to sew. Considering the situation Mata found herself in, one might conclude that the odds of the Tashiro relationship flourishing would have been quite small. But flourish it did. Masaki and Mata raised seven children. In later life, when her husband was plagued with arthritis, Mata successfully managed their farm.

Katsubei Sakaguchi first met his picture bride, Hisano, when she arrived in Seattle. Together they settled into a Platteville farm as sharecroppers. Their marriage, too – if not their farming at first – would thrive. The next year they moved a few miles south to work land near Wattenburg. From 1915 to 1918, the Sakaguchis farmed east of Brighton. Such frequent moves were common trials in the sharecropper's life. The Sakaguchis made a final move into farm ownership in 1919, when they bought a 160 acres south of Brighton where other Japanese families had already settled.

Katsubei Sakaguchi sharecropped on farmland near Wattenburg, Colorado. Vegetables were transported to the Kuner Canning Company processing plant in Brighton in this horse-drawn wagon in 1914.

A Brighton area farmer by the name of Shunpei Momii described another daunting aspect of farming along the Front Range: "I get hailed out year after year," he complained. "What an unlucky person I am. I am sick of this life!" Momii happened to be part of a group visiting the Platteville home of George and Toku Nakata, where they had gathered to hear about the activities of Denver's Buddhist Temple, founded in 1916. Upon hearing Momii's discouragement, Toku Nakata was reminded of the comfort she had received from her faith while living in Japan. She said, "While in Japan we used to gather at least once a month to hear the Dharma...the teachings of the Buddha. If possible, how wonderful it would be if we could have a *Kyudokai* [a religious gathering] at least once a month here in America." Her comments led to an initial meeting in the Fort Lupton home of Yasokichi Takaki, on August 6, 1922.

Two years later, when the Nakatas moved to Brighton, they called on Zentaro Goto, the president of the BJA, and his two brothers to discuss the establishment of a Kyudokai there. After discussions with other Issei in the area, they helped organize a Kyudokai, held a month later in the Goto home in Henderson. Reverend Ono from Denver delivered the first address to the area's Issei who were settling into an increasingly comfortable and permanent lifestyle.

Along the South Platte River in Adams and Weld counties from Henderson to Platteville, others in the generation of Japanese bachelor immigrants were also transitioning into farm ownership. And settling into married life. Children followed, naturally. Lots of them. It was natural for the Issei couples to have large families, as it was for all farm families. Kids were an asset because so much work had to be done by hand. Horses still pulled plows; but farmers and their kids planted, tended, and harvested the cabbage, beets, and other vegetables. Helen Okada wrote this of her parents' generation: "They were all farmers between Henderson and Platteville. And they expected the kids to help! We used long hoes to weed and thin every day. Later – simple cultivating with a single horse. Lots of walking!" These labor-intensive practices continued for decades and, to a lesser degree, remain the norm today. Ron Ida harvested cabbage during his childhood in the 1940s and 1950s. He said that at harvest time each head of cabbage had to be handled three times in order to move them from the field to the wholesaler. "We used to cut the cabbage by hand and throw each head onto a farm wagon, take it into the farm yard, and toss each head onto a truck. When we had a ten-ton load of cabbage, we would take it to the market, and we'd have to pitch it again from the truck." Harvesting sugar beets was equally labor-intensive, with weeding, thinning, and watering done throughout spring and summer. Harvesting beets involved gently unearthing them with a special pitchfork and lopping off the greens from each beet, called topping, with a specially designed knife. Despite the uncertainties of weather and the intensity of care required, the lowly sugar beet, along with the cabbage, grounded and sustained an entire generation of Brighton's Japanese immigrant farmers.

CHAPTER TWO:

The Children

W hen Katsubei and Hisano Sakaguchi bought their farm in 1919, they already had three children. A fourth – daughter Fujiyo, nicknamed Fudge – arrived the same year. The Sakaguchis would have ten kids over a period of seventeen years: the first born in 1914, the last in 1931. Today, unsuspecting drivers crisscross the Sakaguchi farm site when passing through the intersection of Highway 85 and E-470. A description of their farm is representative of the other Issei farms in the area. The house and yard were circled by cottonwood trees, as well as practical chokecherry bushes and apple and plum trees. Off a ways stood a shed for "odor-rich" *tsukemono*, cucumbers and other vegetables pickled in wooden *shoyu* barrels. A barn quartered two mules and eight horses. They pulled wagons that transported the farm's vegetable crops to the Kuner Canning Company plant in Brighton.

Close to the house, Sakaguchi designed and built a traditional Japanese bath house, a *furoba*. In it he installed a one hundred-gallon galvanized tank on a hollowed-out, cement floor. Wood burned in a fire pit beneath the tank heated the bath water. Bathers actually washed themselves before entering the tank for a soothing soak in the hot water. They had to submerge a floating wood pallet, by standing or sitting on it, to avoid burning their feet on the tank's hot metal floor. Every Saturday night was *furo*: bath night. Two of the Sakaguichis' daughters recalled the homestead with "great nostalgia," though the house had only three bedrooms for the twelve of them. As the family grew, the sleeping arrangements became understandably more complicated. Fudge Sakaguchi wrote:

> Mom and Dad had one room… Mas [the youngest] slept with Mom and Dad. The [four] girls had one room and two of the boys slept at the foot of our beds. Kay and Kez had the other room…It was a very cozy home…We had no electricity or running water. We had to use an outhouse. We read books by a kerosene lamp and we had to go about 500 feet to a pump to get water. I remember carrying two pails at a time and would carry at least ten buckets in a day if not more.

Yet there were refinements in Fudge's childhood, too. For example, she played the violin. The kids walked two miles to the Henderson School; in winter Dad sometimes accompanied them, carrying all of their books. A few years later he would drive them to school when bad weather hit, if his "old jalopy" started. The school had only four classrooms, with two grades in each room, but it played an important role. "School opened our social contacts to kids from the district," wrote younger sister Yayeko (Yaye). "School was our social life too." Years later Bob Sakaguchi would add to his aunt's observation, saying, "Even the early Nisei, my father's generation, had to deal with the language barrier. It wasn't until [they went] to grade school that they really learned how to speak English" since in most of their homes only Japanese was spoken. Often, only the Issei men learned English, so they could conduct business within the community. The women, who worked within the confines of the home, could get along without it. Throughout the 1920s and into the 1930s, Nisei names appeared on the class rosters at Henderson Elementary: Chikuma, Goto, Igata, Katayama, Nakata, Noriyuki, Sakaguchi, Tashiro.

The Nisei generation's assimilation into the community would be a factor in the future when they formed the BJAA as young adults. "They had been to public school," Hisa Horiuchi wrote, "and had formed bonds within the greater Brighton area community." Schooling was not without its challenges, however. Satoshi Chikuma was dismissed from his elementary school for not speaking English. Satoshi, known as Harry, was the first child of Gotaro and Yoshi Chikuma. Younger brother Bill remembered that consistency was also a problem. As sharecroppers, their parents moved almost every year, so the kids had to adjust to a new school each fall. Bill Chikuma started first grade in Brighton but then progressed through a litany of the area's one- and two-room schools: Hazeltine, Brantner, Barr Lake, Independence, and Fort Lupton.

Gotaro Chikuma and his bride Yoshi, pictured here in their wedding photo in 1912, settled in the Platte River Valley early in the twentieth century.

Yoshi Chikuma and three of her children (left to right), Inez Asano, Sam Norio and Bill (Willie) Satsuki, in 1921.

In the public schools, community connections reached across the racial divide. At Hazeltine Elementary, George Masunaga, who would be BJAA's first president, became "best buds" with Benton Murray, whose parents farmed down the road from the Masunagas. In fact, George and Benton became "partners in crime," collaborating on a number of childhood shenanigans, according to Benton's son Glen. On one particularly eventful school day, Masunaga and Murray lost their recess privileges for some infraction of the rules and were confined to the empty classroom following the lunch period. The school's custodian had left a ladder there, which gave the boys the notion to open a beckoning trapdoor in the classroom ceiling. While exploring the school's attic, one boy slipped and put his foot through the plaster ceiling. Both scurried back down the ladder. To camouflage the damage, they found a large roll of art paper, taped a piece of it over the hole, and swept up all evidence of plaster dust from the floor. The teacher, evidently, did not immediately notice the patch job – the ceiling being quite high – or at least she never pinned the damage on the pair.

During another lunch recess, the two boys crossed a wooden plank set as a temporary bridge over the Fulton irrigation ditch running near the school – in order to explore the territory beyond, no doubt. When recess ended, their teacher sent some girls across the plank to call the explorers back to class. But before the messengers could return, the boys impulsively pulled the plank onto the bank, stranding all of them from access to the schoolyard. Both the explorers and the messengers had to make quite a hike along the ditch to find an alternate crossing – and gaining a good deal of extra recess time in the process. Glen Murray's own memories of Masunaga jive with the stories told by his dad. "Everyone knew George," Murray said. "He had a personality that you might say was *bubbly*. He was fun to be around and was always joking." Those were qualities that would serve him well in adult leadership roles.

At Christmas time, Hisano Sakaguchi would buy each of her kids' teachers a small gift. "Mom was so generous and kind," Fudge Sakaguchi said. "She was an excellent cook, cooking for every event and family gathering." Yaye Sakaguchi recalled in poetic detail the "kinder, gentler time" of their childhood and the connection the kids felt to nature:

> I remember the signs of spring - the smell of lilacs, Johnny jump-ups on the roadside, meadowlarks singing, doves cooing...carefree summer days, bare feet, spending an hour lying on a cot watching the white puffy clouds go by. One of the things I remember vividly while growing up were the electrical storms...The air is dry so the electricity of lightning and thunder really crackles. I remember a horrendous lightning bolt lightening up the sky and outlining the cottonwood trees against it.

"I guess we were poor," she concluded. "Everybody else was in the same boat. We didn't notice. Did I ever feel disadvantaged? No, I did not."

Not all of the Issei were farmers, of course. Tanemi Katagiri left his farm near Nagano, Japan, in 1903 and found work in the U.S. at a general store in Portland, possibly S. Ban and Company. When he moved to Colorado, he was put in charge of shipping and sales at S. Ban's Denver branch store near the intersection of Twentieth and Larimer Streets in downtown Denver. S. Ban was Shinzaburo Ban, a fellow immigrant. In the 1920s, Katagiri sold clothing, personal items, and familiar Japanese foods to Brighton's Japanese families and to miners in the mountains of Colorado. His wife, Miyo, was the store's bookkeeper. The Katagiris then moved to Henderson to open their own general store and gas station. They lived in rooms in the back of the building where they raised a family. The Katagiri store became a social gathering place for the Issei in the neighborhood, including Junzo and Kiku Tanaka, Sakuju and Sada Sato, and Yaichi Hishinuma. At the store they all caught up on the local news, planned fishing trips and mountain hikes together, and played a board game called Go.

Tanemi and Miyo Katagiri, in their 1916 wedding photo, worked at the S. Ban mercantile store in Denver before starting their own business.

The Katagiri store and gas station in Henderson, Colorado, became a gathering place for the Issei farm families in the area.

Baseball became a passion among the younger Issei men. On any given summer Sunday in the 1920s, as many as four Issei baseball games were played on diamonds from northern Colorado to the Arkansas Valley. Especially hard hit by the "baseball fever" was Fort Lupton where two teams were formed, one on each side of Highway 85. The west-siders were the Higashi Yamatos; the east-siders, the Nishi Yamatos, touted as the better of the two. As proof of Yaye Sakaguchi's label of the era as a "kinder, gentler time," the *Rocky Mountain Jiho* reported: "On the baseball field, summer Sundays were furnace hot. Sweating young Issei players were polite and their fellow fans respectful; not a sign of a jeering howl at questionable plays or an umpire's decision."

One eager young player from Wattenburg was Sadao Naka. He had played the all-American game on his high school team back in Fukuoka. (Baseball had been introduced in Japan as early as the 1870s.) Of course, baseball season falls at the most inopportune time for farmers tied to cultivating and irrigating crops in the summers. The demands of the fields were strong, but then so were the calls of the infield and outfield. Sadao Naka's Sunday dilemma was described by a Denver journalist and is worth quoting:

> Even on Sundays, summer was a time when even a tolerant father was reluctant to allow his son to go off to play ball. On one Sunday when one of the Yamato teams was to play a crucial game and his joining them was "absolutely necessary," his adamant father, Kakichi, refused him permission. Then, to the rescue of the frustrated but obedient son came [team manager] Chiataro Okamoto... He respectfully requested Naka senior to let his son play. He received a reluctant consent.

On another Sunday, young Naka assured Dad that he would finish his irrigating chores after that week's baseball game. Upon returning to the farm, he was "horrified to see precious ditch water over-flowing onto the public roadway." Complicating the situation further, he was both "mortified and grateful" to see his mother trying to stem the overflow. In addition to Fort Lupton and Brighton, the first Issei baseball league in Colorado included teams from Ault, Greeley, Longmont, and the Arkansas Valley. Harry Hokosano was himself a fan. He rooted for the Denver Nippons.

Baseball fever lasted well into the next generation, but for the Nisei kids, a less enjoyable summer activity was about to be imposed. "Around 1922, the [members of the Brighton

Nihonjin Kai] took a vote on whether or not to have a Japanese school," Jane Tashiro said in a 1981 interview. "The ones wanting a school won and we went to Japanese school in Fort Lupton during the summer." George Masunaga explained the parents' decision further:

> Denver, Ft. Lupton, and Brighton all had their own Japanese associations, separate organizations. And yet the purpose of the organizations was all about the same: to give the young kids a good Japanese background. So they formed Japanese language schools. Denver had Japanese language schools after the regular school for an hour or two every day. We in Brighton finished our elementary studies and started Japanese school the next day for the whole summer.

During the regular school year, "dreaded" review classes were mandated every Saturday to keep the kids from forgetting what they had learned during the summertime. Most of the teachers were college men from Japan who were studying at Denver University, including brothers Kyoshiro and Ryokichi Tokunaga. Most could not afford to go home between semesters but could make "a good living" then as teachers in the outlying language schools. In 1927, the BJA bought a building near the South Platte River to house its school. A former roller-skating rink known as the Brighton Pavilion just northwest of the intersection of Highways 7 and 85, it was used for social events as well. *Fukushu Kai* was the name parents chose for the building, *fukushu* meaning a place to review lessons or to learn.

One hardworking teacher during the late 1930s was D.U. law student George M. Koshi. "We all strove for assimilation in the general community," Koshi said, "[but a] trend to ignore our ethnic background headed the Japanese language toward extinction among the Nisei. The Issei parents were alarmed at this trend and established the Japanese school in order to preserve the Japanese language and...culture...and maintain better communication between parents and children." Bob Sakaguchi held a childhood misunderstanding that illustrates the language divide within families. "Growing up, my [Issei] grandparents living on our farm spoke only Japanese," he said. "My mother and father could speak both English and Japanese. My sister and I could only speak English. So I thought that as you got older, you started to pick up Japanese, but then as you got even older you forgot how to speak English."

Parents like Miyo Katagiri also taught summer school lessons. Daughters Emi, Mami, and Fumi attended for eight years. Former student Bill Chikuma remembered well the sights and sounds inside the classrooms. "We read books out loud," Chikuma wrote, "as we held the books out in front of us." Then, commenting on the quality of the recitations, he added, "It sounded like a haunted house."

Businessman John T. Horie, also a strong advocate of assimilation, opposed the basic tenet behind the Japanese language schools. He was quoted as saying, "The children's parents - all born in Japan and forbidden by law to become American citizens - all expected to eventually return to their homeland. They wanted their children to be ready when the time came." That seems an odd assessment, considering the advancements being made by the Issei in business and agriculture. It seems more likely, during the late 1930s when war with Japan loomed as an ominous threat, that as a group they anticipated forcible ejection from the homeland they had adopted. Horie clearly felt that they were better off in America and that they should remain here. When Congress passed the McCarran-Walter Act in 1952, he became a tireless advocate of permanency, teaching classes to prepare the Issei in Northern Colorado for citizenship, even before he obtained his own.

Despite his opposition, Horie himself taught Japanese in schools in Ault and Kersey in Weld County. His personal story sheds light on his opinions about the language schools. While studying English literature at Tokyo University, Takashi Horie hoped to become a college professor in Japan. Meeting the daughter of an American missionary family, however, changed his career trajectory. In 1924, while doing graduate work here in the U.S., Horie married the missionary's daughter, Chloe Ann Jaeger. Her father gave Takashi the name John. It sounded more American. The Depression prevented Horie from completing his literary studies, but he forged a career as executive secretary of the Colorado Japanese Growers Association. Of the Nisei, he noted that not only were they citizens by birth but "culturally too they were Americans. They would never have been able to make a life for themselves in Japan. They belong here."

Bob Sakaguchi's dad, Kay, was one of the kids compelled to spend part of his summer studying the Japanese language. He and George Masunaga were one day apart in age. And again George obviously did his best to turn his school experience into an adventure. Masunaga, laughing at the memory, told a story about being taken to summer school on the back of a one-ton, converted truck, a REO Special, where as many as twenty kids would squeeze aboard. (Bill Chikuma remembered a White farmer in the area referring to the truck disparagingly as a "cattle truck.") Kids being kids, behavior on the rides to and from summer school was less than prim and proper. In reaction to the natural rowdiness of his young passengers, the truck owner rigged up a magneto to generate an electric current. He connected it by wires to the seats on the truck bed where Masunaga and his buddies usually sat - so he could give them a jolt when they got too rowdy. In anticipation of the next day's shocking ride, the boys came up with a scheme of their own. "One of them said, 'Have you got an old rubber inner tube at home?' So we cut pieces and put them in our pants. The driver would push and push the switch, but nothing happened. Eventually he dismantled it." Sharing the "bus" driving duties were George Uyemura, Eddie Okada, and teacher Koshi. When the truck wasn't doing double duty as a school bus - or a disciplinary machine - its bed was restored for hauling loads on the farm. Some sources say that before the Brighton school was organized some kids had traveled to the Fort Lupton classes in style on the train, taking advantage of passenger rail service available at the time north of Denver.

Other Brighton teachers were Suekichi Matsunaga, Nobuzane Tsumura, and Harry Chikuma, who as a kid had been dismissed from Barr Lake Elementary for not knowing English. In addition to George Masunaga, summer school students included future BJAA members and officers Mike Tashiro, Jim Tochihara, Harry Fukaye, Jack Uno, and Harry Ida. Close to one hundred alumni of the Brighton Japanese language school gathered for a reunion in 1985, with teacher

George Koshi in attendance. His address to the group gives a look into the classroom deportment of his students in the late 1930s and early 1940s. He recalled his Nisei students as having been "innocent and mischievous," especially the latter, evidently. After finishing law school at D.U. in 1940, Koshi joined the Army and was recruited for intelligence training, later serving as an instructor in the program. "My teaching experience at Brighton certainly came in handy," he said, "but [in the Army] I didn't have to bang on the desks with a stick or throw erasers. A threat of court martial kept all students in line." Bill Chikuma remembered laughing with his buddies in class at one *sensei* (teacher) who had a hole in his pants. The teacher, one of the cash-strapped college men who was no doubt humiliated and angered by the laughter, restored order to his classroom by isolating the rascals. "He took us to the teacher's quarters in the building," Chikuma wrote, "hit our hands with a ruler, and left us to stand there the rest of the day." Once the teacher returned to the classroom, of course, the boys took it easy by sitting on the floor until they heard him returning, when they stood up and managed to look as if they had been compliant with his punishment in the interim. Considering the level of parental involvement in the Brighton language school, it is likely that word from a teacher of classroom behavior prompting a thrown eraser or a popped ruler would have garnered additional punishment from an Issei parent.

The BJA building, the former roller rink, was renovated to include three classrooms, a stage and, out back, the requisite baseball diamond. Some functions held at Fukushu Kai, such as athletic contests in judo, sumo, and kendo, probably garnered more interest among the Nisei kids than did summer classes. It was home to banquets and kabuki performances, the organization's business meetings, as well as funerals and other religious ceremonies. A reporter for the *Jiho* encapsulated the plain, barnlike building's appeal: "Its functions consistently drew enthusiastic crowds. One felt there the community's pulse."

Students and teachers from Brighton's Japanese Language School prepared for a pageant in 1924. The two sword-yielding warriors (upper left) are future BJAA leaders George Masunaga and Kay Sakaguchi.

Students and teachers of Brighton's Japanese Language School posed for school photos during many summer sessions, this one during the 1930s [detail].

Frank Tanaka, the first to hold the office of BJA president, was followed by a succession of willing leaders: Minejiro Nakasugi, Juro Goto, Katsubei Sakaguchi, and Magoki Masunaga. In 1924, young Frank Nakata, the son of an Issei, was elected president. Just twenty-one years old and only seven years in the U.S. himself, Nakata was also a "first generation" American. In those early years of the BJA, when the Nisei were mostly toddlers and teens, Nakata was "a stalwart" in the association. His official service in the role of president ran through 1930. Nakata, whose military career in Japan had been superseded by the call of family in the U.S., was "an even-tempered, stabilizing influence in community affairs, and an observant optimist" at a time when the Issei generation was producing a number of able leaders. And "service," then as now, was a key word. But BJA members helped each other without official urging from an association. They stood by each other at the birth of a child, in sickness, and at the time of death. Nakata would call the BJA "a supportive community."

Japanese Americans from Hawaii to the Great Plains continued to swat at the baseball bug throughout the Depression of the 1930s, when the sport was still truly America's National Pastime. "Whoever wants to know the heart and mind of America," wrote Jacques Barzun, an historian of ideas and culture, "had better learn baseball." Young Nisei men didn't need to have a scholar tell them that. So strong was their interest that today an entire website is dedicated to the Nisei baseball phenomenon. "Baseball has been integral to the Japanese American experience," proclaims NiseiBaseball.com. It provided more than just "a way of escaping for a few hours on a Sunday afternoon from hard labor in the fields and cities." Baseball actually "helped to build community; it helped to nurture pride." Even more so, baseball gave the Nisei "something in common with neighbors who often wanted little to do with them; it gave them a way of becoming 'American.'"

In Northern Colorado, there were two Nisei baseball leagues: the Young Buddhists' Association (YBA) and the Young Men's Association (YMA). Brighton boys played on teams in both. Their goal was to win a Labor Day tournament at the end of each season. Hank Shibao played for Brighton's YBA team. He learned the art of catching from his brother George. "One thing I learned was to guard your plate," wrote Shibao. "I got toppled quite a few times. I used to peg the ball to second, and I put it in there. Players noticed, so they quit stealing second." Shibao recalled a few other teammates: Herb Onodera, at shortstop; George Doi, the only lefty on the team; John Kurachi; Wes Koyano; Bill Chikuma; and manager Harry Shibata. Pitcher Tom Shibao threw fast balls and had a good change-up, too.

Members of a Brighton baseball team (left to right), Kyoshiro Tokunaga, who later became a Buddhist minister, a Mr. Ujifusa and Shinkichi Tokunaga, circa 1930.

The roster of a 1936 Brighton Young Men's Association baseball team was filled with many future leaders of the BJAA. Top row (left to right): George Shiyomura, George Misunaga, Kay Sakaguchi, Lander Ito, umpire Duke White, manager Richard Takamine and Jim Imatani. Bottom row (left to right): Masato Tashiro, Tagus Murata, Jess Masunaga, Tom Tochihara and Harry Tazawa.

Players in the summer of 1939 enjoyed the competition of the "All-American Sport." Top row (left to right): Tom Momii, Yoshio Naka, manager Mr. Motooka, Bill Chikuma, Noble Muroya, Sandao Naka, Sam Chikuma, Harry Shibao and Jim Muroya. Bottom row (left to right): Harry Eguchi, George Toshi Shibao, Sam Naka, Tom Shibata, Toshi Muroya, John Kurachi and Haruo Katayama.

Of course, baseball, school, and family were not the only institutions holding the Japanese Americans together. After uniting in 1922, Brighton's Buddhists continued to meet in their homes for Kyudokai services until 1938, when Issei farmer Shunpei Momii pushed for the construction of a permanent temple. Momii – the farmer whose proclamation "I am sick of this life!" had first impelled the local Buddhists to organize – had obviously found comfort in his Buddhist faith and wanted to give the Kyudokai a visible presence in Brighton. Despite opposition from some in the White community, ground was broken for a temple on August, 4, 1938. Members did most of the construction themselves at the temple site on First Avenue, including digging out a basement with farm equipment pulled by teams of horses. Volunteer carpenters came from seven families: Chikuma, Mizunaga, Katayama, Momii, Motooka, Onodera, and Shibao. The shell of the temple was completed by the spring of 1939, but a dedication ceremony did not take place until February 18, 1940 after the interior was finished. The country at large had undergone seismic changes since the first Issei had settled in Colorado. But throughout the "Roaring" 1920s and the Great Depression of the 1930s, the Japanese families in the Brighton area continued to expand and assimilate. Farmers, it is often said, are less impacted by a bad economy than are wage earners in the cities. Consumers buy groceries, even when their incomes are down. And, of course, the Issei farmers already knew how to deal with hard times. Farmers' routines remained routine; baseball remained hot; and kids continued to walk to school. Kioko Kawakami is named as the first Japanese American to graduate from Brighton High School, in 1928. She was followed by the Imatani sisters, Mary in 1929 and Helen in 1930. (The sisters would become Mary Tokunaga and Helen Okada after their marriages.)

Miyo Katagiri (seated) taught classes for the Brighton Japanese Language School during the 1930s. Her daughters Emi, Mami and Fumi attended summer classes there for eight years.

The Katagiri family, and friends, posed for a picture in front of their business before sending mother Yoshi and daughter Fumi off on a trip to Japan, in 1938.

In 1939, a national telephone directory of Japanese Americans listed forty-seven families in the immediate Brighton area. That same year, Republican Ralph Carr was sworn in as Colorado's governor, an otherwise inconsequential detail had it not been for the courageous stance Carr would take on behalf of the rights of Japanese Americans. In Europe that year, Germany invaded Poland, starting a war that would engulf the entire world. In 1940, Germany's air force began deadly night-time bombing raids on London. Here in the U.S. there were loud and insistent voices debating the advisability of the country becoming entangled in the European conflicts. The events on the world stage were noticed at Brighton High School, where the speech class debated the very timely proposition: "Resolved, that every male citizen of the United States should be required to have one full year of military training before attaining the age of twenty-one years." No report on who won that debate.

The high school's student newspaper, the *Brightonian*, bore witness to the Nisei teens' full involvement in student life. A front-page article noted that Seiji Horiuchi "placed fourth in poultry judging and sixth in poultry and egg judging at the state FFA contest held at Fort Collins." In fact, four of the eleven farm kids who attended the state convention were Japanese Americans, including George Uyeda, Bill Doizaki, and Johnny Sakurai. In Fort Collins, they heard a presentation on "agriculture and national defense and their correlation." Looking forward to graduation, the student journalists published senior quotes and "wills" in their newspaper at the end of May. Hatsuko Tochihara chose a few optimistic lines of poetry as hers: "The world is happy / The world is wide / Kind hearts are beating on every side." She willed her "shyness" to Helen Tanaka. BHS graduated forty-six seniors in the class of 1941.

For the new term in the fall of 1941, the Brighton marching band was outfitted with new uniforms, in a "semi-military" style. Under the headline "A Good American Citizen," the editorial board of the *Brightonian* told fellow students, "The war in Europe has proved to us that we must have a lot of moral courage to withstand the hardships that a war brings." With uncanny foresight, they also encouraged "tolerance, good will, and thoughtfulness among one another." They added, "Loyalty, honesty, sincerity, and respectability all go together to make us the kind of citizens that America needs today." A short news item –ominous in hindsight – reported that two BHS graduates were back in town on furloughs from the Navy. Both "brought back interesting experiences and tales of places they had visited." At least one of them was to report to the West Coast again in September of 1941 for a return voyage to their base – at Pearl Harbor, Hawaii.

For years on the West Coast there had been attempts by Japanese Americans to unite in the formation of advocacy groups. Finally in 1929, the Japanese Americans Citizens League (JACL) took hold. By its own proclamation, JACL is today the "largest civil rights organization in the country focused on Americans of Japanese ancestry." It was not until 1938 that a Denver chapter was initiated. Called the Mile-Hi Chapter of the JACL, its roots grew within the Nisei generation. Twenty-one-year-old Shimpei Sakaguchi, the third child of Katsubei and Hisano, was elected the chapter's first president. His contributions are still remembered on the Mile-Hi

JACL's website. "Dr. Shimpei Sakaguchi," it reads, "set the path and leadership that has endured and prospered."

Beginning in the winter of 1940-1941, there was fear among Colorado's Issei generation about the worsening relations between Japan and the U.S. That fear was addressed at a two-day meeting in March, 1941 by members of a Denver group called the Japanese Association of Colorado (JAC), which Bill Hosokawa described as "a loosely knit organization that was part benevolent society, part social association, and part struggling watchdog over Issei rights." Those in attendance included Shimpei Sakaguchi's dad, Katsubei. Both had become quite the organization men. JAC members discussed the possible negative effects on the Japanese American community should a war break out and prepared for "crisis management." They discussed the role of education and Japanese language schools in the lives of their children, the need for keeping cash on hand in case their bank accounts were frozen by the government, and "the possibility of mob violence against Japanese in Denver if tensions in Asia continued to escalate." Prompted by their discussions, the Issei in attendance vowed to "apprise state and local officials of their concerns." Individuals who are excluded from full participation in society often find solace and acceptance by banding together. When the language barrier made social interaction difficult for the Issei, they formed their own Japanese organizations. When Anglo society looked at them and their Nisei children with fear and suspicion, they again sought a voice and a degree of influence through organization. Exclusion and inclusion are flip sides of the same coin, of course. Spurned by the larger society, Japanese Americans found a welcoming hand from those with familiar names and faces.

In March of 1941, members of the Japanese Association of Colorado, made up largely of Issei generation immigrants, met at the organization's Denver offices to discuss the looming conflict between Japan and the U.S. Many Brighton area residents, including Katsubei Sakaguchi, participated.

But their organizations were not formed for the purpose of demanding equality or fighting for rights, even nonviolently as did the NAACP founded in 1909. Early attempts to organize among the Japanese Americans, such as the JACL movement begun in California, were more predicated on conversation with the larger society, apprising "state and local officials of their concerns." And persuading by example. Even in the internment camps of WWII, the Issei would organize, not to protest their imprisonment but to maintain as much normalcy and routine in their daily lives – especially in the lives of their children – as possible under the harsh conditions they found themselves in. "You gotta hand it to our folks," said Nisei Bob Sakata. "The first thing they did after internment was organize the camps into blocks and elect leaders within each. The second thing they did was form schools." When the Brighton women formed the BNWC in 1948, they initiated public service projects. When the BJAA formed in 1950, the Brighton Nisei men hoped to display their loyalty to the country through concerted community action, giving back to the very community that still resisted their presence. Their service activities and community contributions predated the massive marches and demonstrations of the civil rights movement by a decade.

The Issei and Nisei living in Colorado at the beginning of the Second World War were not subjected to internment. The Issei in Colorado, however, were as determined as their counterparts held in the camps to maintain a degree of normalcy for their children during the war years. Many Issei even refrained from disclosing to their children and grandchildren the harsh news of the imprisonment of 110,000 West Coat Japanese Americans. Their reticence may have sprung from the Japanese trait referred to as *gaman,* the disciplined acceptance of one's lot in life. Joanna Sakata admitted, "The first time I heard about 'camps.' I thought they were like summer camps or church camps." The first time Bob Sakaguchi heard about them was some twenty-five years after the fact, in a professor's lecture on American history, which Sakaguchi found quite a jolting revelation. When he asked his parents about the camps, they said nonchalantly, "Oh, yeah, that's not important." *Gaman.*

In October, 1940, the JACL held a conference in Denver. The main speaker for the event was Colorado Governor Ralph Carr. Two months after the Pearl Harbor attack, Carr addressed the vicious contempt being aimed at Japanese Americans. In the official newspaper of the JACL, the *Pacific Citizen,* he wrote, "This is a difficult time for all Japanese-American people. We must work together for the preservation of our American system, for the continuation of our theory of universal brotherhood."

With storm clouds on the horizon, the JACL attempted to add to its numbers and beef up its potential as an advocacy group. However, there was little enthusiasm outside of Denver for forming other local chapters. The executive secretary of the national organization at the time was Masaru (Mike) Masaoka. After passing through Northern Colorado on a recruitment drive for the national JACL, he wrote, "The integration of Nisei in many inland communities was well advanced, and many felt no need for JACL." Fort Lupton residents eventually formed a local chapter; Brighton residents never have. With some alarm, Masaoka also found little awareness among the Nisei about the break-down in relations occurring between Japan and the U.S. so fervently discussed in Denver that spring and fall – a shocking lack of engagement in world affairs, considering the date of his first recruitment meeting in the state: Friday, December 5, 1941.

The same weekend, Brighton High captured the second state football championship in its history, beating Burlington 7 – 0. On Saturday, December 6, George Koshi taught a routine review session at the Brighton Japanese School. It would prove to be the final Saturday session of the Fukushu Kai. Forty-four years later, Koshi would be able to address his former students light-heartedly about the required Saturday sessions: "You must have wished that such a 'horrendous practice' would be discontinued. Well, your secret wish was instantly granted when Pearl Harbor was attacked the following day. All

Japanese language school activities then came to a screeching halt."

It is an understatement to say that Japan's attack on the U.S. had an immediate, negative impact on all Americans of Japanese ancestry. Beginning on Sunday, December 7, 1941, the Issei and Nisei living in the U.S. were lumped together with the military force of Japan. They were suddenly "The Enemy," cunning and cruel and hell-bent on world domination. It would be an obstinate stereotype, one that would take a generation to refute.

At the fiftieth anniversary celebration of the BJAA, George Masunaga gave a speech that included his memories of Pearl Harbor and its immediate aftermath. "The executive secretary of the [BJA] came to our house every day for a week," Masunaga recalled, "saying that we must dissolve the Japanese Association." Masunaga's father, Magoki, was president at the time. He reassured the secretary that the FBI and other government agencies already knew the peaceful intentions of the BJA and would not cause problems for members. "Just stay calm and wait," he advised. Fortunately, no one bothered the membership, despite the fact that their President Magoki Masunaga lived close to the Rocky Mountain Arsenal; so close, in fact, that overzealous government agents might have viewed the location of his farm as suspicious. George Masunaga's comments about Pearl Harbor, coincidentally, were made in October, 2001, just one month after another horrendous, surprise attack on America on September 11.

Magoki Masunaga's comments aside, the Brighton Japanese Association was disbanded soon after the attack on Pearl Harbor. A brick was thrown through a window at the

Buddhist Temple. The YBA and YMA baseball leagues went on hiatus. When finally granted the right, most of the Nisei baseball players would volunteer for the truly deadly game playing out on the battlefields of Europe.

CHAPTER THREE:

War and Beyond

After the attack on Pearl Harbor, Katsubei Sakaguchi instructed his family to remove all Japanese language books and magazines from their home and burn them. On the Chikuma farm, Grandma hid everything associated with Japan. In Henderson, Miyo Katagiri hid a photograph in the attic of the living quarters behind the family store. It was a formal portrait of her brother dressed in his Japanese Navy uniform. Around Brighton and across the U.S., Issei families destroyed similar mementos, in fear of being linked to the enemy. Their actions were a reasonable response to an explosive situation. Across the country, angry and vile outbursts were being leveled at the country of Japan and, by association, at all Japanese Americans.

President Franklin Roosevelt reacted to America's anger and suspicion with Executive Order 9066. It instructed the secretary of war to forcibly remove all "aliens and non-aliens" from parts of the country where they might pose a military danger to America by conspiring with Japan. That meant all 120,000 Issei and Nisei in the Pacific Coast states of California,

Oregon, and Washington. A Brighton Nisei named Thomas Kido apprised Governor Carr of his personal frustrations with the order in a letter. "In peaceful times we are called fine people, fine Americans," Kido wrote. "In wartime we are now called, en masse, a suspicious, traitorous, and dangerous element. Must we have white faces to be Americans at all times?" At Brighton High School, the Nisei students found society's stereotypes and attitudes impinging on their lives following the outbreak of war, as witnessed by a student-written editorial in the *Brightonian* just a month after the Pearl Harbor attack:

> After the eventful Sunday, Dec. 7, 1941, some of the remarks aimed at Japanese students to the effect that they were pro-Japanese in sympathy, had absolutely no justification. The public as a whole is quieting down now but if conditions in the war grow worse these unjust accusations will probably flare up again. Remember that the Japanese in this school are as good Americans as any of us, perhaps even more so, and it is wrong to make them feel like outcasts. So let us take this as a gentle reminder that we young people are here to learn – to learn that the only worthwhile and the only successful aim is to make this a better democratic world for ALL people.

During a period of "voluntary evacuation," 10,000 Japanese Americans managed to move inland from the West Coast before mandatory internment was executed. Many found temporary homes in Colorado, largely due to comments made by Governor Ralph Carr welcoming them to the state. At

BHS, twenty new students enrolled for the fall term of 1942, quite an influx considering that the entire graduating class of 1941 had numbered forty-six. Many of the new arrivals were Japanese Americans, including "Alice Kumada...formerly of San Jose High School in California [and] Esther Fushuro...formerly of Los Angeles." The trend continued throughout the fall semester, and eight more students enrolled by December. Shingo Umene, transferring from Alameda, California, was asked by a student journalist about his initial experiences at BHS. He answered with typical teenage understatement, saying, "So far, so good."

But 110,000 Japanese were unable or unwilling to relocate. They were interned – imprisoned really – at camps built by the U.S. government across the West. Sixteen-year-old Bob Sakata was one of them, along with his dad, his brother Harry, and sisters Mitsie and Fusi. They were first forced to live in a horse stall at a former racetrack south of San Francisco and later under extreme desert conditions at a camp called Topaz in Utah. Sumiji Horii – the grandfather who had inspired young Lindsay (Kline) Auker to adopt a new middle name – was interned in Poston, Arizona. (There, within the confines of Camp One, he met Hideko Mizuguchi. They would marry and spend their honeymoon in Camp Three.) Sam Sasaki and his wife, Yoshiko, were sent to the Jerome War Relocation Center in southeastern Arkansas from their home in Long Beach, California. It was the last camp to be opened and the first to be closed. In June of 1944, Sasaki moved his family to Henderson, Colorado, when the camp closed. Through hard work and sacrifice, he was able to begin farming there. Using farm practices he had learned in California, Sasaki soon became known locally as the "Celery

King." Other "evacuees" from the Pacific Coast settled also settled permanently in the Brighton area, such as the Kitayama and Sakata families.

Despite the enmity aimed at Japanese Americans, World War II brought out a spirit of national unity and involvement that has not been duplicated in this country. Students did their part, too. Girls in the homemaking classes at BHS, including Helen Tanaka, knitted sweaters to donate to the Red Cross. In a 1942 speech, President Roosevelt suggested that high school students could best serve their country by helping farmers harvest vitally important crops to alleviate the farm labor shortage caused by the war. A good percentage of the Brighton students answered FDR's call to the fields, digging and topping sugar beets that might otherwise have rotted in the ground. School was officially dismissed for two days in Brighton to encourage that involvement. Of course, a good number of the "volunteers" were farm kids and would have been expected to help in the harvest anyway.

In a strange coincidence, German soldiers being held as prisoners of war near Brighton were also recruited to harvest crops for Japanese American farmers such as Nagahiko Mizunaga who grew sugar beets. In a family history, his son Keiji (Charles) remembered that the prisoners of war were always hungry and that he would occasionally buy them donuts. Alley Watada, who lived on a farm near Fort Lupton, told a similar story to the Densho organization. "[D]uring the war labor was short, so I remember bringing prisoners, German prisoners, on the farm to help harvest potatoes." Watada's mother had heard that meals provided by the U.S. military were sparse so she made baloney sandwiches for each captive harvester. "We were instructed not to feed them," Watada said, "so my mother…asked us to leave [the sandwiches] near the field where they knew it was, and tell 'em it's there, but it was not real visible to outside people." On the Chikuma farm, Grandma boiled ears of corn in a washtub for the POWs. Was this collusion with the enemy? No, just common decency. Compared to the awful conditions being endured at the same time by 110,000 loyal Japanese Americans in internment camps, the treatment of German troops by the U.S. government – and by local JA farm families – was civil and humane. And farm work, far from being a punishment, gave the captive soldiers relief from the boredom of confinement.

At the same time, interned Nisei such as Harry Sakata were recruited from Utah's Topaz camp to work in the beet fields of Idaho. Shinkichi Tokunaga employed Japanese workers from the internment camps to harvest lettuce on his farm near Granby, Colorado. His wife, formerly Mary Imatani, cooked for the men and washed their clothes as well as working with them in the fields. Tokunaga's daughter, now Joanna Sakata, marveled at her mother's efforts, asking, "Can you imagine doing this with no electricity or running water while raising six children?"

Many Brighton residents came from German ancestry, including dairy farmer Bill Schluter, whose generosity gave Bob and Harry Sakata their start in Colorado farming. One of the cruel ironies of the war was that Japanese Americans were viewed with wholesale suspicion while German Americans were not, although in 1940, it is estimated, they comprised close to thirty-five percent of the entire population. Japanese Americans that year made up only one percent of the population of California.

Harry Hatasaka reflected on his personal roller coaster of emotions on the war's home front in an essay for a writing contest sponsored by Brighton's Junior Chamber of Commerce. Addressing the topic "America Goes to War: What it Means to Me," Hatasaka wrote:

> When I heard that Japan had ruthlessly and treacherously attacked several United States possessions, a sudden grip of fear seized me. I was mostly afraid of capture by the American government because I am Japanese. I have now lost that fear, due to the fact that the United States is a free country. I am very grateful for the fact that I live in America, which is one of the very few nations of the world that is free from fear and want.

For Brighton teens and adults alike on the home front, life went on, although with personal adjustments and sacrifices. Aside from the rationing of consumer goods that affected all Americans, travel was the only additional restriction for Japanese Americans in Colorado. "The only restriction was to have a permit to go more than fifty miles," John Horie wrote. "Just about every weekend I'd go to get a permit to go trout fishing. They never questioned me."

Brighton's Nisei generation progressed through the local school system. Representatives of the war years included Ruth Chikuma and Sumie Tashiro, who graduated from BHS in 1940; Hatsuko Tochihara, who graduated in 1941; Seijii Horiuchi in 1942; Emi Katagiri and newcomer Bob Sakata in 1943. Some sixty years later, Hisa Horiuchi would tell a group of BHS students that during the war years at the school she was "very discriminated against for being Japanese, but never bullied." Nevertheless, she got involved in student life, including the school pep club, and graduated in the spring of 1945. By then the influx of Japanese American students from the West Coast had made a noticeable impact. The BHS class of 1945 consisted of one hundred students, almost double the number in the class of 1941.

Before the Pearl Harbor attack, more than five thousand young Nisei were serving in various branches of the U.S. military. In the anti-Japanese hysteria and paranoia that followed, many were abruptly discharged. As a group, all other Nisei men – potential recruits – were barred from military service when the government reclassified them 4-F (unfit for military service) or worse, 4-C (enemy alien), though they were clearly U.S. citizens and the need for recruits was crucial to the very survival of the country. Their sudden exclusion from service was a crushing blow. Daniel Inouye of Hawaii remembered well the government's decision. "That really hit me," he said, expressing the sentiments of many in his generation. "I considered myself patriotic, and to be told you could not put on a uniform, that was an insult. Thousands of us signed petitions, asking to be able to enlist." At his death in 2012, Inouye was the most senior member of the U.S. Senate.

In the fall of 1942, Ralph Carr ran for a second term as Colorado's governor. A majority of voters, however, were displeased with him – based solely on his support for the rights of Japanese Americans – and turned him out of office.

During the first three years of the Second World War, victory for the U.S. on either front - in Europe or in the Pacific - was anything but certain. As the need for military manpower became increasingly urgent, President Roosevelt himself authorized the formation of an all-Nisei military unit to be called the 442nd Regimental Combat Team (RCT), saying, "No loyal citizen should be denied the democratic right to exercise the responsibilities of citizenship, regardless of ancestry." The situation was not unique in American history. During the Civil War, African Americans were excluded from serving in the Union Army for the first two years of conflict. In 1863, the governor of Massachusetts "squeezed permission" from the War Department to recruit African American men for a single regiment. Willing volunteers filled two. Even then, African American soldiers were limited to service in segregated units such as the Fifty-fourth and Fifty-fifth Massachusetts Regiments led by White officers. A prohibition against African Americans continued through the end of WWII.

When Secretary of War Henry L. Stimson announced in January of 1943 that the Army would again accept Nisei recruits, more than twelve hundred of them nationwide signed up for military service almost immediately. The obvious irony for many young Nisei men was that volunteering for military service was a means of escaping internment, a Get-out-of-jail-NOT-so-free card. By the end of the war, a wave of 17,600 Japanese Americans had served in the U.S. military. The Brighton Nisei were among them. During just one recruitment period in the spring of 1944, seventy-seven area men made the commitment. Below an attention-grabbing head-line – "LATEST INDUCTEES FROM ADAMS COUNTY ACCEPTED LAST WEEK" – the *Brighton Blade* published a list of the individuals. Sixty-five had Japanese surnames. Seeing those names listed so prominently in the press must have had a positive impact within the community. But not all those listed were actually inducted. At least eight, according to Goro Sakaguchi, were the oldest sons of farm families and therefore deferred from military service, including Goro's oldest brother, Kay. Feeding the nation was also deemed crucial to the war cause.

The local men who were deemed eligible reported to Fort Logan, south of Denver, for physicals and required paperwork and were officially inducted in July. "About three hundred of us," said Goro Sakaguchi. He and his brother Ray were assigned to different platoons in the same company of the 442nd RCT. The brothers were shipped to Camp Shelby, in Mississippi, for basic training, as was Hawaii's Daniel Inouye, who commented on the experience: "We'd only heard about the lynching [of African Americans in the South], but to our surprise these people were very good to us. We were invited to weekend parties, and for the first time in my life I danced with a White girl." He added that back at the base the other soldiers were not so welcoming, but "the problems were minimal because they could see we had a whole regiment!"

In Brighton, the Sakaguchis watched five of their six sons leave for war; the Shibaos watched five leave. Bill Chikuma also went. As a teenager, he had been sent to Japan to attend high school, where he graduated from the Shugaku Dan Nichi

Bei Home, in Tokyo. "I lived at school," he wrote, "which disciplined me, and I learned Japanese. I had a good time playing basketball, and studied judo and kendo." In fact he earned a black belt in judo. He returned to the States just before the beginning of the war and served in the 442nd RCT from 1942 to 1945 in Italy, Germany, France, and Czechoslovakia, rising to the rank of staff sergeant in command of a platoon. In Europe, he earned a Purple Heart. After the war, Chikuma returned to farming near Brighton and later, though he had moved to Denver, shared his skills teaching judo classes to Brighton kids.

Bill (Willie) Satsuki Chikuma was one of the local Nisei volunteers who served in the 442nd Regimental Combat Team in Italy, Germany, France and Czechoslovakia between 1942 and 1945. He rose to the rank of staff sergeant, was wounded and awarded the Purple Heart.

Issei generation Japanese Americans like Yoshi Chikuma had to register with the government during WWII as resident aliens. On this 1942 form, Chikuma made her mark below her photo, as witnessed by her Nisei neighbor Masato (Mike) Tashiro.

Tom Doi was an eighteen-year-old junior at Fort Lupton High School when he decided to enlist. He played football there, but because his coach had already gone to war, Doi felt no compulsion to stay in school. In Europe, Doi's leg was blown off just below the hip by a German mortar shell. "I'm not bitter," he said after the war, "because it was my share in something that had to be done. If I had to do it over, I'd probably go again." By war's end, the 442nd RCT and its units had become the most heavily decorated single combat unit of it size in U.S. Army history. Nisei infantrymen of the regiment earned 9,486 Purple Hearts. Two of the Nisei volunteers from the Brighton area were killed in combat: Taka Ito and George Kawano.

Ralph Carr's successor as Colorado governor was John Vivian. He too would deal with Coloradoans' unjustified fears of the Japanese Americans in the state. Those fears were felt most strongly in Adams County, because an increasing number of successful JA farmers and businessmen were buying real estate there. "Seven pieces of property have been purchased by five Japanese buyers since the outbreak of the war," cautioned the *Brighton Blade* in January, 1944, "including three pieces of business property in downtown Brighton." Brighton Mayor J. W. Wells called the situation "alarming" and, with a like-minded delegation, called on Governor Vivian for help. He told the governor that Brighton residents were fearful of "agricultural and business exploitation by the Japs." Wells was also a state senator. He introduced an anti-alien land law bill to the Colorado legislature, similar to those on the books in other states, that would have prohibited ownership of real estate by "aliens ineligible for citizenship." In other words, the Issei. Governor Vivian was advised that the state's laws in no way prohibited land ownership by non-citizens. After much debate, the issue was placed in the hands of the voters in a fall referendum to amend the Colorado Constitution. The JACL and other influential state organizations lobbied against the measure. Surprisingly in the post-Pearl Harbor hysteria, the proposed Anti-Alien Land Law was defeated statewide by a margin of 15,500 votes. The tide of prejudice was ebbing. The sacrifices and obvious patriotism of the Nisei soldiers was having an impact not only on the battlefields of Europe but also in the voting booths of Colorado.

The volunteer spirit displayed by the Nisei soldiers was remarkable and inspiring. That spirit also predicted community involvement in civilian life after combat ended. On the list of those determined to enlist in the spring of 1944 were the names of four men who would become the founding officers of the BJAA: Tom Tochihara, George Masunaga, Kay Sakaguchi, and Masato (Mike) Tashiro. Sakaguchi, Tashiro and others were deferred to work on their fathers' farms. Their patriotism and loyalty under fire – both literally and figuratively – remained constant and would be channeled into public service through the BJAA in civilian life. Roy Mayeda was a sterling example of that impulse to serve. Mayeda graduated from what is now Colorado State University with a degree in chemistry. In 1941, he was drafted by the Army, one of the rare exceptions who was not drummed out of service after Pearl Harbor. He served with the medical unit of the 6th Army. He rose from private to captain during a five-year military career and, although he never fired a shot, earned two battle stars in the South Pacific. Back in civilian life, he served a term as president of the Mile-Hi JACL in 1953 and then took many roles with BJAA, including five presidencies over the next four decades. He also served on the Brighton City Council. Mayeda Park on west Jessup Street in Brighton was named in his honor.

George M. Koshi, the Japanese school teacher turned soldier, had been sent to Washington, D.C., on a special intelligence assignment at the War Department. When the war ended in 1945, he was selected as one of sixty from the department to serve in occupied Japan, where he took part in the trials of Japanese accused of committing war crimes. He arrived on a "cold, damp, and weary November day." His description of the defeated country and its people is heart wrenching:

Japan looked even more desolate and Godforsaken than anything I had heard or read. People were dressed in rags, with their eyes looking vacant. The sad part of it was that they all looked so much like our Issei parents. They were just hopelessly and desperately trying to survive. Journalists labeled them the "People who forgot how to smile."

Willie Kiyota, who left his family's farm near Fort Lupton for Europe, had also seen haunting sights during the war. "Some things," he said, "a fellow just can't forget." Kiyota was wounded three times and earned an officer's commission on the battlefield. But he looked instead to the future. After the war, he told the *Denver Post* that he "preferred to remember the joy of coming back home and the satisfaction a man gets from turning Colorado soil and watching things grow."

When the main body of the 442nd RCT was returned to the U.S. in the summer of 1946, it was paraded through Washington and reviewed by President Harry S. Truman. The president told the Nisei, "You fought not only the enemy, but you fought prejudice - and you have won." Truman gave the veterans an additional challenge, saying, "Keep up that fight, and we will continue to win – to make this great republic stand for just what the Constitution says it stands for: the welfare of all people all the time." That "fight" on the home front was yet to be won. The Brighton area Nisei men –both the war veterans and those who had served at home – would take up Truman's charge, in part, with the founding of the BJAA.

Mike Tashiro cultivated cabbage on his 160-acre farm in 1940.

In 1946 the Sakata homestead included a Japanese bath house, the white building in the lower right with soot on its outer wall.

A truck full of cabbage on the Kagiyama family farm was ready to take to market in the fall of 1946. Sitting on top was Ed Tashiro.

The Kagiyama family harvested onions together in 1948.

Kenso Kagiyama tended cabbage on the family farm in 1949.

CHAPTER FOUR:

Assimilating, Organizing

Having weathered the war, Nisei teens and twenty-somethings again turned their attention to sports. But the girls were no longer willing to sit on the sidelines at athletic contests watching the boys swing at baseballs and shoot hoops. The Nisei Women's Athletic Association (NWAA) was formed in 1946 to make softball fields and basketball courts available to the "young ladies" in the Denver area. Games were played in the big city, so again, many young Brighton women like Emi Katagiri and sisters Rose and Helen Tanaka took to the road. JACL's monthly *Denver Bulletin* covered the action on the diamond. In a lively piece of sports journalism, a reporter wrote a jargon-filled summary of the post season softball game between the league's All Stars and the season's championship team, the Debonnaires. The game did not end well for the season champs, but Brighton players on the All Star team showed their metal:

The combined strength of the NWAA All Stars proved too much for the League Champion in the final exhibition game as the Stars flashed to a 9 - 3 victory with Masako Murata, steady Brighton chucker [pitcher], working a five-hit mound chore.

The All Stars piled up a 5-0 lead in the second inning when Peg Taiguchi waited out the offerings of Debs' pitcher Rose Endo and was driven in by the Brighton short center, Rose Tanaka. Successive singles by Toshi Okamoto, Virginia Ito and Helen Kimura brought in four more runs.

Murata registered two successive strikeouts in her defensive half of the opening inning and was never in hot water except in the sixth and briefly in the seventh [inning], but the Stars had such a large lead the faltering Debonnaires fell far short in their abbreviated rally.

The post-war rush to marriage took precedence over softball, of course, but one player even postponed her honeymoon to play the last nine innings of the season. The *Bulletin*'s reporter ended the game summary with praise for newlywed Rosa Higashi, who had been Rosa Sato just the day before. Sato/Higashi "relieved pitcher Endo to nip the second All-Star spurt in the fifth inning but not before three runs were chalked up." Could these women athletes have been any more American? Following a second post-war sports season, the NWAA hosted a joint awards banquet with their male counterparts, the Denver Nisei Basketball League. NWAA player/president Helen Tanaka presented the winning teams with gold basketball trophies. Then there was dancing to the "tinkling tunes of Dan Axel's orchestra."

Young women from Brighton traveled to Denver in the years immediately following the Second World War to play competitive softball. This team, pictured in 1946, included future Softball Hall of Fame member, Nancy Ito (front row left).

The Nisei college kids from Henderson were also making the trek to Denver to join the reincarnated Mile-Hi chapter of JACL, which had suspended all functions for the duration of the war. George Masunaga – being referred to as the group's "most eligible bachelor" and later a "perennial bachelor" – was president for at least one term and edited the *Denver Bulletin*. The Katagiri sisters joined. Mami was on the small staff of the *Bulletin*. Emi and Mami were elected officers. Many others were equally attracted to the organization in the post-war years. Membership in Denver's chapter jumped from 137 in

1949 to 500 in just a few years. It would grow to be the largest chapter in the national organization, which in 1951 had 10,000 members. One year almost fifty new members were signed up from the Brighton area alone. And no wonder, with so many Brighton folks active in the group's leadership.

Minoru Yasui was also an active JACL member. He had made a name for himself in Portland, Oregon, in the early years of the war when he challenged the constitutionality of a city curfew targeted only at people of Japanese ancestry. As Adam Schrager wrote in his book *The Principled Politician*, the young lawyer had "filed a legal challenge to [the curfew's] legality, sent word to the U.S. Attorney's office and the FBI, and went out into the streets to be arrested." And he was. Under the peculiar wartime circumstances of 1942, breaking curfew had been no small infraction for a Japanese American on the West Coast. The twenty-five-year-old Yasui was sentenced to a year in prison and stripped of his citizenship, which also meant the loss of his license to practice law. He served nine months of his sentence in prison – in solitary confinement according to one report – and was then moved to the Tule Lake internment camp in northern California to serve the balance of his time. At Tule Lake, he was reunited with his family, already in internment there. With the help of the American Civil Liberties Union, Yasui appealed his arrest and imprisonment all the way to the Supreme Court, which also ruled against him, calling his arrest justified as a "military necessity." He was able to leave Tule Lake in 1944 and subsequently moved to Denver where he was befriended by former Governor Ralph Carr. After petitioning for a reinstatement of his license to practice law, Yasui took the Colorado bar exam and made the highest score in the history of the state test. Carr expressed pride in his new friend, saying that Yasui exemplified "greatness as a man and as an American."

In the fall of 1950, Ralph Carr passed away. A friend of the state's Japanese American community, Carr was eulogized in the JACL *Bulletin*: "Ralph Carr loved people for what they are. It made no difference if they were of a minority group. We shall miss him." Years later a statue of Carr was erected at Sakura Square in Denver to commemorate his contributions to the JA community. A similar statue was erected nearby of Minoru Yasui.

The social lives of the Nisei high school and college crowds returned to a state of normalcy. George Masunaga, who had been a downhill skier since childhood, organized weekend runs to Arapahoe Basin. He offered to teach neighbor Emi Katagiri to ski. "I'll teach you to ski," Masunaga said, "in exchange for a ride to the slopes." Katagiri, Masunaga, and four of his buddies enjoyed many winter days on Colorado's up-and-coming ski slopes. "I was kind of the little sister in the group," Katagiri – later Chikuma – said. At the end of the day, the guys would send her to the car with instructions to drive back down the pass and wait on the shoulder of the highway below the maintained ski area – so they could enjoy one final, out-of-bounds run to the bottom of the mountain.

Like the rest of the nation, the Nisei settled into marriage in record numbers in the late 1940s and early 1950s. Couples did their part for the nationwide "baby boom" that would so noticeably increase the U.S. population during the next twenty years. Most JA singles found spouses within the comfort zones of their local Japanese communities, following tradition rather than contesting societal sanctions against interracial marriage. Joanna Tokunaga's parents moved their family from Grand County, where they grew lettuce, to the Front Range. "My parents decided to move to Brighton because they wanted their children to become acquainted with other Japanese," she said. "I think they were concerned that we needed to marry within our race and since there were not too many young Japanese in Granby, the chances of that happening were pretty slim." In 1956, Tokunaga would marry her Brighton neighbor, Bob Sakata. The inclination to marry within the Japanese community seems not to have implied an attempt on the part of the Nisei to isolate themselves from the mainstream society. Just the opposite. American citizens from birth, they nevertheless had to seek recognition and acceptance from and assimilation into White society. Despite the obvious personal sacrifices made for the country by the Nisei veterans of the Second World War, Japanese Americans still faced the racial discrimination that had stymied them during the war. It blocked their efforts to fully integrate with the larger community, even in Brighton. "We were very much despised," Don Tanabe told a Denver news reporter. "We had to prove to the others in the population that we were good people." Even civic organizations such as the Elks refused JAs membership. In hindsight, for years those organizations lost the energies and contributions of a segment of society that was eager to contribute and to prove its worth.

The young wives were also excluded from full community involvement. The war had broadened women's expectations by opening new employment roles for them outside the home, but the Nisei women of Brighton, first and foremost, felt an underlying need for socialization. To that end, in 1948 they formed the Brighton Nisei Women's Club. One of the BNWC's first members was the former Fudge Sakaguchi, who had married Mike Tashiro. Thinking back to the group's founding, Tashiro wrote, "A few of us women just got together for fun and just to talk." No dues were expected from the five or six original members, but the women soon established a more formal structure. Tashiro's sister-in-law, Katherine Sakaguchi, was elected the BNWC's first president. From Nebraska, Katherine had married the oldest Sakaguchi son, Kay. Sisters Mary Tokunaga and Helen Okada were also among the original members, with Okada serving as president during the club's second year. Mami Katagiri, later Mami Ito, was another early member. Known for her organizational skills, Katagiri was elected the group's third president. They met once a month in the basement of the Buddhist Temple in Brighton. Socialization meant talk, and the talk – one can surmise – spanned a gamut from the familiar frustrations of family to the unknowns of an unfolding new decade. One thing was off limits, however. "We did not talk about political topics," said Tashiro. Another early member admitted that talk of "local news" was popular. "Boy, could they gossip!" she disclosed.

As the BNWC grew in membership, a formal constitution was drawn up to state a more lofty purpose: "To promote the welfare and culture of the area's Japanese Americans." Joanna Sakata remembered Saturday morning classes being offered, when "much of the Japanese culture was passed on." Members shared their talents in presentations on Japanese cooking and crafts. They taught how to arrange flowers and make Christmas tree ornaments. Deko Shibao demonstrated how to make miniature Japanese umbrellas from a "special decorative paper"

– the wrappers from cigarette packages. Some fifty to sixty packs went into the making of each umbrella! Supplies of the paper were plentiful since nearly "everyone smoked in those days." The final products, folded into a variety of delicate patterns, still display a definite handmade quality – and reveal a great deal of patience on the part of their creators – with no hint of their tobacco-product origins. The unique ornaments adorned Emi Katagiri's Christmas tree beginning in 1950, when she married Dr. John Chikuma.

Joanna Sakata provided a sampling of the presentations made later during her term as program chair: Florence Nakata and Haruko Sasa held classes for several weeks, teaching other members how to make traditional futon comforters and *zabutons*, cushions. Various cooking classes were held on the proper methods of making sushi and cutting sashimi. A Japanese chef from Denver showed the group how to make *oyako donburi*, rice with chicken and egg sauce. They also learned how to make a cookie-like confection called *yaki manju*, a skill which Joanna and group of other members used for several years, making large amounts for the bake sales held during the Chow Mein Dinners. Mary Chikuma, Taeko Morimitsu, Mary Tokunaga, Alice Horii, and Atsuko Kagiyama would prepare the *azuki* beans for the dish ahead of time, which, Sakata said, was the most difficult part of the project. Over the years, the BNWC also invited outside speakers to address the group on other practical topics. One of those was local attorney Ed Brown who spoke on estate planning.

A hallmark of the BNWC was the willingness of members to share leadership duties. During the forty-one years of its existence as an autonomous organization, thirty-nine different women served as president. Only two served a second term, and those terms were years apart: Emi Chikuma in 1970 and again in 1988 and Rose Tanabe in 1953 and 1989. Their initial fundraiser was a simple Christmas cookie sale. The decorated goodies were cut in the shape of Santa Claus. Later, members shifted their efforts toward service projects. Rose Tazawa, club president in 1956, remembered holding potlucks for the Issei, making a speech in Japanese to the group, which was difficult for her since she was not fully fluent in the language.

Early on, the BNWC was approached to cater lunches and banquets by other organizations. When Bob Sakata was head of the local Soil Conservancy District, he asked the women to cook for the group's annual banquets, which were attended by 300 to 500 people. They were then asked to cater lunches and banquets for occasional events in Brighton like the John Deere Company's sales show and the annual dinners held by the American Pride Fertilizer Co-op and even a dinner at the First Presbyterian Church, which featured Japanese culture as its theme. Occasionally, the women held bake sales and craft bazaars in the old Public Service Company building on Main Street, which also put their skills in the public eye. When Colorado was being considered a possible site for the Winter Olympics in the 1970s, the BNWC was even asked to cater a pre-Olympics event at the old May Company department store building in downtown Denver.

The women were making a positive, noticeable impression in town. At first they used their own family plates, silverware, and glasses to serve diners, and their own flower vases to decorate tables. "In those days, paper plates were a no-no," Emi Chikuma said. "Our tables were beautifully set." As their catering services became more popular, the club invested some of its profits in table services. They earned a reputation for their tasty and efficiently served dinners. "They were the best cooks in town," said Bob Sakata, "and the cheapest." In 1960, when Ruby Nikaido was BNWC president, the women shared their culinary talents by publishing a cookbook. Their first effort contained a modest ninety-six recipes. It was nevertheless well received and frequently consulted.

By May of 1950, the Brighton Nisei men finally organized. Taking their example from the Mile-Hi JACL and the BNWC, no doubt, they formed the Brighton Japanese American Association and began sponsoring their own social events. The first were square dances at the Brighton Buddhist Temple, which were quite the rage – and fodder for the *Denver Bulletin*. "Square dancing is quite a popular fad in Brighton these days," the newsletter announced. "The Jim Imatanis, the Bob Uyedas and the Don Tanabes are classified as the best on waltzes, and of course, our graceful George Masunaga and Lil' Sam Tochihara can do anything." One BJAA dancer was singled out for his impressive moves when readers were asked rhetorically, "Have you seen Harry Shibao jitterbug?" Other couples enjoying the dances were Sam and Josephine Chikuma, Jess and Mary Masunaga, George and May Fujimoto, and Tom and Mildred Tochihara. The need for socialization was being addressed. Other activities followed. Sam Chikuma chaired a fishing derby, offering "many valuable prizes" for the winners. And the men played baseball, with "Tom Shibao hurling and his brother Hank catching," the Brightonians were predicted to be a formidable opponent for any team.

Members of the Nisei generation enjoyed many association- sponsored dances during the 1950s.

The official founding date for the BJAA was November 10, 1950. That was when the Colorado secretary of state's office approved the group's application as a not-for-profit corporation. Named The Japanese American Association of Brighton, Colorado, the group's objectives as spelled out in the application were unequivocal. Using strong, active verbs, the founders stated that BJAA was to be about "promoting the principles of American democracy, bettering relationships between Americans of Japanese ancestry and other Americans in our community, and promoting the welfare of Americans of Japanese ancestry in the community." Note that the word "American" was used four times in the thirty-two-word statement. "Japanese" was used only twice. Whether intentional or not, the wording drove home the central point: This is an

American group. To this day, that emphasis can be heard when longtime member Bob Sakata speaks. There is a definite emphasis in his voice when Sakata mentions "the Brighton Japanese *American* Association." Other than its stated purposes, the BJAA espoused no prescribed religious element, neither Christianity nor Buddhism, although the Buddhist Temple in Brighton was an accessible gathering place for BJAA functions. The group endorsed no political party.

The application for incorporation was signed by nine men whose names would become synonymous with the organization: George Masunaga, its first president, James Imatani, Harry Shibao, Kay Sakaguchi, Sam Chikuma, Hayato Morimitsu, Roy Mayeda, Tom Tochihara, and Mike Tashiro. They were the first executive board. With their nine signatures and the payment of a $6.00 fee, the BJAA was born. Lawyer Min Yasui was asked to write a constitution. It too made clear that the true colors of the BJAA were red, white, and blue. The Preamble declared, "We Americans of Japanese Ancestry, in order to advance our general welfare, to promote the principle of American Democracy, to stimulate a more active participation in civic affairs, and to attain a more harmonious community life, do hereby establish this constitution..."

George Masunaga served two terms as the association's initial president. He was followed in office by Jim Imatani, a farmer and businessman. Imatani and his wife Sumie operated the successful Henderson Pickle Company, which supplied cucumbers to national pickling companies. Eventually all of their children worked there too, as did some of the players from the BJAA baseball team Imatani coached. Roy Mayeda was the third man to serve as president. He would later be elected to the Brighton City Council. Harry Sakata was next in the early line of succession. Sakata also presided over the Mile-Hi chapter of JACL for one term.

George Masunaga was a founding member and first president of the Brighton Japanese American Association.

The assets of the Nihonjin Kai, including the Japanese School property, were transferred to the new, Nisei organization. Fifty years later, when the association was celebrating its half-century anniversary, president Kirk Horiuchi wrote in the BJAA newsletter: "Minutes from a 1950 document [say] that the club was formed as a Nisei gathering club." He quoted Frank Nakata, an Issei, as saying, "The duties of the Nihonjin-Kai have been passed to the Nisei." Horiuchi added, "As I see it, this 'passing of the torch' was the beginning of the Niseis' awareness of their responsibility to continue furthering the honorable intentions of the Japanese Americans in the Brighton area." But the question has been asked, Were there really concerns beyond those for socialization that motivated the formation of an association? Bob Sakaguchi pointed out that within the Brighton community there were lingering fears and suspicions about the loyalties of the Nisei and even about his generation, the *Sansei*, the third generation of Japanese Americans. Counteracting those feelings was one of the founders' "driving forces." A case in point is the experience of Sumiji and Hideko (Alice) Horii, the couple that had met and married in the internment camp near Poston, Arizona.

Almost a full decade after America defeated the forces of Japan, Japanese Americans like the Horiis were still being targeted with discrimination. The couple's attempt to have a house built on Third Avenue in Brighton was publically protested by the residents of the neighborhood, and financing on the home was held up for a suspiciously long time before the couple was allowed to settle in. And the Horiis were not the exception. During the first postwar decade that some look back on with fond *Leave It to Beaver* nostalgia, Brighton even prohibited the Sansei kids from playing baseball with their White friends in the American Legion Pee Wee League. The derogatory term "Jap" was still part of the local lexicon. With the

BJAA, said Sakaguchi, "the Nisei wanted to show the community that they were good citizens...really assimilated into American culture." Of his generation, Sakaguchi said, "We weren't pushed to learn [the Japanese language]. We were taught to assimilate." But, he added, we were also taught to be "proud of our heritage." Those two, intertwined purposes endure within the organization.

Within Japanese culture, of course, honoring one's parents is almost compulsory. That duty was melded into the Japanese American way of life as well. Not surprisingly, one of the first activities sponsored by the BJAA was Pioneer Night, an event staged to fulfill that duty. Amateur entertainment "running the gamut from an old-country sword dance to a comic jitterbug demonstration" filled the basement of the Buddhist Temple on a winter evening in 1951, long before the seventy-two-inch Hi-Def television took dominion over real "family entertainment." Members and their wives showed off an impressive array of homegrown talents. They sang, danced, and played solos for their Issei parents. (One can assume that the BJAA wives had been asked to prepare food and refreshments for the event.) Throughout the program, Bill Chikuma, Roy Kishiyama, Harry Sakata, and H.I. Matsumoto acted out *naniwa bushi*, short dramatizations of Japanese folklore. Businessman John T. Horie was the evening's featured speaker. He made it clear that the night's entertainment was intended to recognize the accomplishments of the pioneers in the Japanese community, especially for rearing their children to be good Americans worthy of the opportunities the country offered. And those opportunities were seized with enthusiasm by the Nisei, a significant number of whom sought college degrees in the professions. Formal education was something that the

Issei generation had forfeited in lieu of raising and supporting families so their children could became doctors and dentists, nurses and teachers, and excel in an array of businesses.

BJAA members helped celebrate the Tri-State Buddhist Temple with a Kabuki performance in 1949.

Linda Hori, Yoko Koyano and Vicki Sakata performed a traditional Japanese dance during a talent program in 1963.

Nadine Kato, Elenor Fukaye, Phyllis Nakagawa and Lorri Huff performed on a Denver television station in 1968.

The pride the Nisei felt for their parents' sacrifices, however, was accompanied by a degree of frustration on their behalf. The U.S. government continued to deny the Issei the opportunity to gain citizenship. Veteran Tom Doi shared his personal frustration with journalist Bill Hosokawa. "Take my father, for example," Doi said. "Why is he still denied the privilege of becoming an American citizen although he has lived more than half of his life in this country? This is land that Dad and Mom helped develop. They raised us kids on it and taught us to love it." The Platte Valley, with its view of the mountains to the west, reminded Doi of the Po River Valley in Italy, where he had been wounded during the war. "Mom died on this soil, and Dad probably will be buried in it when his time comes. And still he isn't really of it, because technically, after all these years, he's still an alien. The law won't allow him to become a citizen."

In 1952, Congress addressed that frustration. It passed the McCarran-Walter Act, also known as the Immigration and Nationality Act (INA), which at last gave the Japanese American "pioneers" the right to pursue citizenship. The Issei in Adams and Weld Counties clamored for preparation classes in anticipation of taking the naturalization test. Businessman John T. Horie was willing and able to help them and many others. Not yet a citizen himself, he volunteered his time teaching preparation classes in Brighton, Fort Lupton, Greeley, Longmont, and Denver. "I was like an old-time Methodist itinerant preacher," he wrote later. In Brighton his students segregated themselves at tables in the basement of the Buddhist Temple – women on one side of the room, men on the other. Each came prepared with a steno pad and pencils. They reportedly asked their teacher to repeat each bit of information several times, to fix it in their notes and in their memories. Most of the students, of course, were farmers. At age eighty-one, T. Kubo was the senior member of the Brighton class. He had retired just two years earlier from raising cabbage and onions, which he had done since his arrival in the area in 1905.

John Horie - always dressed in suit and tie - prepared his students for tough civics questions like, What does the Fourteenth Amendment to the Constitution say? How can the Constitution be amended? What is the Monroe Doctrine? Nisei – and citizen – Sam Tashiro joked that after his mom took Horie's class she knew more about the U.S. government than he did. Regarding the time and talents he had given to the classes, businessman Horie said humbly, "There's more to the day than work." By the time the crash courses in America history and law were completed, Horie had enabled at least 250 Issei to gain citizenship.

President Harry Truman actually vetoed the McCarran-Walter Act, considering it un-American and discriminatory *by not going far enough* in welcoming those from Eastern Europe who were still suffering from want and oppression after WWII. Truman's veto was overridden by both houses of Congress. As Truman had foreseen, the act was used over the years to bar members and former members of the Communist Party from entering the United States, even those who had not been associated with the party for decades. Parts of the McCarran–Walter Act remain in place today, although sections of it were overturned by the Immigration and Nationality Services Act of 1965.

Along with their much-desired citizenship, many of the Issei also received official recognition for the Americanized names by which they had long been known. Judge Christian D. Stoner, who administered the oath of allegiance for the Adams County ceremonies, said of Teizo Hatasaka, "As long as everybody calls him 'Frank,' he should be permitted to adopt the name legally." Teizo left the courthouse officially a citizen and officially Frank Teizo Hatasaka. Junzo Tanaka and Mitsuhei Mayeda of Henderson became Joe and John, respectively. The McCarran-Walter Act enabled some of the earliest Issei pioneers in the Platte Valley to receive their certificates of naturalization: the Sakaguchis, the Nakatas, the Tashiros, the Chikumas, and merchant Tanemi (Fred T.) Katagiri. For Katsubei Sakaguchi the chance to swear his oath of allegiance to the United States came on June 2, 1954. His oath was witnessed by Haruko Sasa, "housewife," and L.M.

Smith, "farmer," probably a neighbor, though, judging from the surname, not of Japanese descent, and, more significantly, a sign of Sakaguchi's good standing with the larger Brighton community. Sakaguchi's good name would stand, too. Where his naturalization petition allowed for a change, Sakaguchi checked "no name change desired."

A group of Brighton's Isseis stood to be recognized for the first time as American citizens at the Adams County Courthouse after taking the oath of citizenship in 1953. At far left is businessman John T. Horie, the volunteer teacher who helped them prepare for the naturalization exam. At far right is Judge John Stoner who presided over the ceremony.

Gotaro Chikuma's certificate of naturalization, which documented his U.S. citizenship, was issued on August 30, 1954 by the Eighth Judicial District Court in Greeley, Colorado.

Early in 1952, the Brighton Nisei Women's Club planned a fund-raising bazaar to be held at the Buddhist Temple. After months of preparation, the women had an inventory of handmade items to sell, including embroidery pieces, tea towels, aprons, and pillow cases. The BNWC's Oriental Bazaar was "highly successful," according to President Hazel Tani and committee chair Mary Tokunaga. Over 600 shoppers attended, generating net proceeds of $1,700. The entire sum was designated for the building of bleachers and restroom facilities at a new baseball park to be developed on land purchased in 1951 by the BJAA at the corner of North Twelfth Avenue and Longs Peak Street in Brighton. The purchase had been made possible by the sale of the former BJA Japanese Hall, which had been passed on to the BJAA after its founding. Despite the prohibitions placed on Japanese American kids by local sports leagues, baseball would continue to be a part of their summers.

A year later, the women of the BNWC began what would become the organization's defining activity, bringing a degree of acceptance to the Japanese community in Adams and Weld Counties that it had not been able to achieve previously. The Shrimp and Chow Mein Dinner, started under the presidency of Rose Tanabe, would be the first annual offering in what is now a long tradition. The men of the BJAA were called on for help with the dinner. It continued as a joint effort of both organizations, though in the opinion of some, the women were the backbone of the event and remain so. It's an opinion that many senior members still acknowledge, however tacitly, with a reserved smile and a nod. Of course, the men did their part. Ken Horiuchi recalled learning how to peel shrimp properly in preparation for dinners, a task he learned from Emi Chikuma and Florence Nakata. For the first few years, diners were met at the door by Rose Fujisaki, who had a knack for seating folks "strategically" to accommodate the growing crowds showing up for some Japanese cuisine at venues that soon proved to be too small. The purpose of the Chow Mein Dinner is twofold, according to Bob Sakata. "It allows us to preserve the culture and share it with the community. And as a fundraiser it enables us to pay back to the community through charitable donations." The shrimp and chow mein dinners remain a local hit.

The women of the BNWC held their First Chow Mein Dinner at the American Legion Hall in Brighton, a facility that the event quickly outgrew.

Minoru Tagawa (left), Jim Kiyota and Gene Watada greeting diners at the front door.

The first duty for volunteers is serving tea.

Voulunteers prepare all of the food for the Chow Mein Dinner.

Katherine Sakaguchi laughing about the amount of flour covering her apron

Dennis Kitayama (left) and Don Tanabe peeling shrimp.

Lindsey Auker (left), Kathy Watada and Linda Kline tending the take-out line.

Working in the kitchen

Volunteers on the serving line are kept busy throughout the afternoon.

Christopher Horiuchi stirring the chow mein.

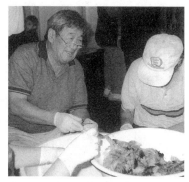

Food preparation

Calvin and Donna Noguchi working together.

Deep frying shrimp

Food preparation   Kirk Horiuchi and Wayne Berve
                                working over a hot stove

BRIGHTON J.A.A. - 1960

ANNUAL

CHOW MEIN-SHRIMP DINNER

BRIGHTON 4-H BUILDING
DINNER SERVED FROM 4:30 TO 8:00 P.M.
Saturday_____April 2
ADULTS $1.75   CHILDREN $1.00

Bob Sakata with the trailer rig used to store cooking gear and other supplies from year to year.

CHAPTER FIVE:
Leading and Giving

Within the first few years of their founding, the BNWC and the BJAA created an active Nisei social scene in Brighton. But when Mike Tashiro took over leadership of the men's group in 1955, he challenged the membership to broaden the scope of their activities. In doing so he enriched the group's culture from within and strengthened its reputation around town. "When Mike got hold of [the BJAA], we became very respected in the community," said Bob Sakata, who was the civics chairman during Tashiro's leadership. "We proved that we were no threat but a real asset to the community." The turnabout came as Tashiro steered the organization toward a philosophy of community service and philanthropy. The tool that would finance this culture shift would be the Chow Mein Dinner. Over the years, it would become a fundraising dynamo. The formula remains a simple one: Enlist a small army of volunteers to prepare a quality meal; Offer it to the community at a reasonable price; Return all profits to the community for the benefit of all residents. In large part, that was Mike Tashiro's vision.

Tashiro was elected president again in 1958 and 1959. His wife, Fudge, served in the same role in the BNWC in 1957. They both took their duties seriously. "During my year as president and the year after, when Mike was president of the BJAA," Fudge Tashiro said, "we used to argue a lot on how the clubs should be run and what the clubs should do. We were both passionate about the clubs and wanted the best for the members." By all accounts, Mike Tashiro was an outgoing man, gregarious and eager to share his affinity for humor. The typed speeches he prepared for association functions are colored with jokes and anecdotes. As master of ceremonies during one formal function, Tashiro joked that a previous speaker reminded him of the little boy who announced after his first day at school that he would not be returning to the classroom. When pressed by his parents for a reason, the little boy said, "I can't read, I can't write and the teacher won't let me talk. So what's the use?" Of her husband's talks before the group, Fudge Tashiro said, "I remember Mike spending hours preparing for his speeches, but he would never practice giving them to me." (Maybe he wanted to keep his punch lines secret.) Together the Tashiros operated a restaurant and tavern on the west side of Brighton called The Terrace Inn. Mike's personality and Fudge's home cooking made The Terrace a popular gathering place. Their customers included officials from city hall and from the county offices in town, and the business friendships Mike generated had positive repercussions for the BJAA and did much to enhance the image of the Japanese American population.

In 1959, Brighton lawyer Orrel Daniel spearheaded a commission to raise funds for construction of what would be the city's first hospital. Daniel asked Bob Sakata to serve as vice president of the group. Their goal was to raise $160,000 toward a building fund. Sakata thought the proposed hospital was worthy of a donation from the BJAA and approached association officers Mike Tashiro and Jim Tochihara with the idea. They in turn made the idea known to the rest of the membership. "For the first time," said Sakata, "I encountered some serious hesitation on the part of the BJAA." The officers had to do some politicking within the association, making many calls on their fellow cabinet members to convince them of the appropriateness of a donation. Their internal campaign was successful. Prior to the next Chow Mein Dinner, Sakata said, "We publicized that all the revenue from the dinner would be given to the hospital." BJAA had made the move from social club to service organization. With a $1,000 donation, it became the largest single contributor to the planned medical facility, as it would be again in 2005 when the Platte Valley Medical Center was built to replace the original facility. The BJAA's gift that year was $15,000.

Caring for those in need has always been characteristic of the Japanese American community, even before the Nihonjin Kai made compassion part of its charter. In 1959, BJAA corresponding secretary Wes Koyano sent a letter asking for help on behalf of fellow member James Kato. Kato had been hospitalized due to a serious accident on his farm, and indications were that he would be incapacitated for a full three months. A very large helping hand was needed. In Koyano's words, "There are 102 acres that must be fertilized, manure to be hauled, spread and plowed in order to get his spring work caught up. Please plan to give a distressed member a hand." A committee had been organized and an "all-out work day" was scheduled for a Sunday in May.

The BJAA's "generous philosophy of helping," however, put the association in desperate need of cash in the early 1960s, according to Bob Sakata. The men took action. "A bunch of the boys, several car loads, about fifty guys," Sakata said, went to Denver and sold blood to Bonfils Blood Center, when that was still a common practice. "I remember Tosh Tashiro passing out afterwards," Sakata joked. About sixty Brighton citizens – including BJAA members – had answered a call for blood a decade earlier when Bob Sakata himself was in the hospital with severe burns over much of his body.

A heartrending example of caring in action occurred in 1984 when a local Japanese American woman was kidnapped. That year Helen Fukui was abducted on December 7. The historical significance of the date strongly suggested a hate crime and put the JA community on alert. Bill Fukui was twenty-one years old when his mother was taken. He recalled that immediately Brighton women showed up to help his family. And they intended to stay as long as needed. "The BNWC women were at our house for weeks…for weeks," Fukui mused. "And to me they were strangers. No other community showed up in force to support my dad and my grandparents and my family like the [members of the BNWC and BJAA.]" Bill Fukui had spent much of his early life in Denver, and he admitted that his mother's abduction exposed him to a thread running through the Japanese American community that he had been unaware of. "It wasn't until that period of time in my life I realized I had missed something growing up. In retrospect, I wish I had been more active with the Japanese community..." he added, "Even today when tragedies happen...this is one of those communities that out of the blue, people just come out of the woodwork [to help]." "No man is an island," wrote sixteenth century English poet John Donne. It could be the beginning of a statement of belief for BNWC and BJAA members. "Every man," Donne's poem continued, "is a piece of the continent, a part of the main...any man's death diminishes me, because I am involved in mankind." Helen Fukui's body was found three weeks after she was kidnapped. Her murder, investigated as Adams County Case #84-11258, remains unsolved.

In 1960, BJAA members built a shelter house in Brighton's Benedict Park. Heading up the construction project was Chuck Shibao, a carpenter by trade who had built and remodeled many homes in the area. Also that year, the BJAA celebrated its accomplishments and acknowledged the volunteer spirit of its leaders with a rather formal ceremony. The Inaugural Dinner Dance was repeated annually and became the social event of the year. At the winter inaugurals, members and their wives enjoyed a meal, officers reviewed the previous year's accomplishments, and all those in attendance welcomed honored guests and witnessed the swearing in of a newly elected leadership team. The inaugurals were rounded out with dancing, and judging from the photographic record, "A good time was had by all." The 1961 dinner was held at the Officers' Club of the Rocky Mountain Arsenal. The commander of the then still-active military base, Colonel Allen, was in attendance and acknowledged by master of ceremonies Mike Tashiro who noted that Allen, coincidentally, had served on General Douglas

MacArthur's staff in occupied Japan following WWII. In introducing the colonel, Tashiro said, "Since he spent some time in Japan, [he] got to know the Japanese people, [and] he always had a warm spot in his heart towards persons of Japanese ancestry."

In 1961 Brighton Mayor Mansewall dedicated a shelter in the city's Benedict Park. The structure was funded and built by members of the BJAA under the supervision of carpenter Chuck Shibao.

Before the evening's meal, Seiji Horiuchi delivered an invocation; afterwards, Roy Mayeda presented awards, and president-elect Don Tanabe took office. Mike Tashiro expressed pride in the BJAA's achievements during the previous year. "The BJAA did carry on many activities for the benefit of its members and the general community at large," he said. "We believe the record is a proud one." Tashiro's closing remarks echoed President John Kennedy's inaugural address delivered earlier the same month. "And now, friends, this meeting comes to an end. So, to you members," Tashiro said, "Do not ask what this club can do for you, but ask What can I do for the club?" He also recited a poem, possibly his own, that was a friendly call to action for other members:

Are you an active member, the kind that would be missed,

Or are you just contented that your name is on the list?

Do you attend the meetings and mingle with the flock,

Or do you just stay at home and criticize and knock?

Do you take an active part to help the work along,

Or are you satisfied to be the kind that just belongs?

Do you ever voluntarily help at the guiding stick,

Or leave the work to just a few and talk about the clique?

Come out to the meetings and help with hand and heart.

Don't just be a member, but take an active part.

Think this over, members. You know right from wrong.

Are you an active member, or do you just belong?

Honored guests were in abundance at the 1963 inaugural, held at the Hilton Hotel in Denver. The event also served as a testimonial, cosponsored by the BNWC, for member Seiji Horiuchi. Horiuchi had accomplished a "first" for the Japanese American community when he won election to the Colorado House of Representatives. He was the first Japanese American elected to a state legislature anywhere in the continental U.S. Colorado Governor John Love attended the testimonial as did Bill Hosokawa, who had risen to associate editor of the Denver Post. In his book *Colorado's Japanese Americans,* Hosokawa wrote that Seiji Horiuchi so impressed Colorado legislators that he was even mentioned as a possible candidate for governor. Horiuchi chose instead to return to private business after two years in the state house. Previously, he had been president of Colorado's Junior Chamber of Commerce (JCC), followed immediately by a term as vice president at the national level. A memorial award in Horiuchi's name is still presented annually to outstanding JCC state chairpersons and program managers. Not surprisingly, Horiuchi had also taken a turn as BJAA president, in 1957.

Roy Mayeda served five different terms as BJAA president.

BNWC members (standing left to right) Josephine Chikuma, Yoshiko Sasaki and Florence Nakata served BJAA members Don Tanabe (left) and Mike Tashiro at the 1955 Chow Mein Dinner.

Don Tanabe (standing) addressed those in attendance at the BJAA's inaugural dinner in 1959. Seated (left to right) are Fudge Tashiro, Mike Tashiro, Bob Sakata and Joanna Sakata.

The newly-installed BJAA officers for 1962.

Colorado Governor John Love (left) Bill Hosokawa, Seiji Horiuchi and
Harry Fukaye took part in the BJAA inaugural dinner in 1963. Horiuchi
was honored as the first Japanese American elected to a state legislature
anywhere in the continental U.S.

1961	President	1962
Don Tanabe		Robert Sakata
	Vice President	
Harry Fukaye		Tom Nakata
	Program	
Robert Sakata		Wes Koyano
	Membership	
Sam Tashiro		Albert Nakata
	Treasurer	
Jess Masunaga		George Okubo
	Recording Secretary	
Tagus Murata		Tagus Murata
	Corresponding Secretary	
Paul Okada		Paul Okada
	Finance	
Mike Tashiro		Harry Ida
	Publicity	
Jim Tochihara		Ken Mizunaga
	Civics	
Seiji Horiuchi		Dr. J. Chikuma
	Property	
Roy Mayeda		Don Tanabe
	Sports	
Jim Imatani		Jim Imatani
Tom Shibao		Tom Shibao

JAPANESE-AMERICAN ASSOOCIATION CREED
We, Americans of Japanese ancestry, in order to advance our general welfare, to promote the principles of American Democracy, to stimulate a more active participation in civic affairs, and to attain a more harmonious community life, do hereby establish this constitution for the Japanese-American Association of Brighton, Colorado.

Brighton

Japanese-

American

Association

Inaugural

Dinner-

Dance

DENVER HILTON HOTEL

January 20, 1962

The program from the 1962 installation of officers banquet.

The Chow Mein Dinner attracted increasingly larger crowds. It is the one event that held the BNWC and the BJAA together over the years. As Joanna Sakata pointed out, "It is a great teaching and learning experience for the members and their families." For many years, Sakata's mother, Mary Tokunaga, chaired the bake sale held in conjunction with the dinners before passing the responsibility on to her daughter. Tokunaga insisted that anything sold at the bake sale had to be homemade, had to look beautiful, and had to taste delicious. After chairing the sale for many years herself, Sakata, in turn, passed the duty on to her niece, Sharon Nishimoto. Net profits from the bake sales held in conjunction with the annual dinners were always high, not only because of the quality of the homemade goodies but also because each member donated two baked items to the sale, including pies, cakes, cookies, and cream puffs. More exotic fare was also offered, including three different kinds of sushi, Japanese crackers, and *manju*, a rice cake. The line for the bake sale often started forming an hour before the doors opened. As a result, annual net profits of the bake sale alone have been between $4,000 and $6,000.

By 1961, the Chow Mein Dinner had to be moved from its original venue in Brighton's American Legion Hall to the 4-H building at the Adams County Fairgrounds, then still located in Brighton. In 1966, a second move to the cafeteria at Vikan Junior High became necessary. Judging from the numbers, diners knew they were getting a good deal for their $1.75 meal ticket. The 1967 dinner served 1,561 guests. A partial grocery list from those booming years indicates the size to which the dinners had grown in just a decade. The list included twenty gallons of Mazola Oil, sixty-five pounds of Gold Medal Flour, eight bushels of bean sprouts, six gallons of *shoyu* – soy sauce – and, not to be overlooked, thirty-five hundred fortune cookies! Many items on the list, then as now, were donated by members and local businesses. When all meals had been prepared and served, there was - and still is - the task of cleaning up. An officer writing in a club newsletter listed the duties that members had agreed to take on, following the list with an emphatically typed reminder: "CLEAN UP COMMITTEE:::::::::: EVERYBODY!!!!!!!!!!"

In 1962, BJAA members were invited by the JACL to become a chapter in its national organization. Members met with legal counsel Min Yasui to discuss the invitation. Yasui emphasized that the Brighton group, if it chose to affiliate, would be able to continue its community service work and to retain its unique identity, and would not be asked to merge with either the Mile-Hi or Fort Lupton chapters. A strong argument for affiliation was the legal representation the national organization could provide in the face of problems that might arise. But disadvantages were identified, too. A portion of BJAA dues would have to be designated for the national organization, necessitating an increase, and recruitment of new members would be mandated and determined by quotas set at the national level. "I think," commented Bob Sakaguchi, "if [BJAA] did join JACL, a lot of their local goals and objectives would probably be diluted. What they really wanted was to be community based." In a straight yes or no vote, the nays held sway for independence, and a continuing local focus.

The governing process within the BJAA has always been a democratic one, albeit a process with no small amount of subtle but positive peer pressure. In 1963, corresponding secretary Shogo Horiuchi alerted members to the annual election of officers at an upcoming dinner meeting to be held at the Terrace Inn. "The nominations for the different offices will be from the floor," he wrote. "You are just as apt to be nominated whether you are present or absent, so you may as well attend and voice your objections, or vote for yourself, and in the meantime enjoy the feast." As an incentive for attendance, the membership had decided to use association funds to pick up the dinner tab, with the polite qualification: "Drinks excluded, of course."

By the mid-1960s, the BJAA consisted of seventy-six members. The Horiuchi name dominated the rolls, with six men from the family holding memberships: Eigoro, Eiji, Karl, Kenzo, Seiji, and Shogo. The leadership being modeled within the organization, and within the BNWC, was duly noted by their children, the Sansei generation. As teenagers, they too got involved in public service. All four offices of the BHS class of 1964 were filled by teens of Japanese ancestry, with Robert Ida as senior class president, Harvey Tashiro as vice president, Joann Masunaga as secretary, and Bob Sakaguchi as treasurer. Sakaguchi joked that he and his fellow officers may have been the only ones willing to take the jobs. But Ron Ida, who was a class officer the following year, said of his fellow JA students: "They had the initiative to do things, like joining clubs." Ida's younger brother and sister also became student leaders in their respective senior years.

All of them were certainly aware of their parents' example; and they could not have been unaware of the ongoing national upheaval that was the civil rights movement and its push for full inclusion for all Americans – regardless of race – in the privileges promised by the Constitution. In Washington, President Lyndon Johnson was insisting that Congress pass civil rights legislation to counteract widespread racial discrimination against African Americans. In Denver, the Mile-Hi JACL officially supported Johnson's proposal. Reverend Martin Luther King, Jr. had visited the city at the beginning of the year, and Mile-Hi's president, Dave Furukawa, attended one of King's mass meetings to show JACL's interest in and concern for civil rights matters. Lawyer Min Yasui, a member not only of JACL but also of the Denver Commission on Community Relations, met personally with Reverend King during his visit.

Following passage of the act by the U.S. House of Representatives, Yasui joined a delegation that called on Colorado's two senators, Gordon Allott and Peter Dominick, to ask for their support when the legislation reached the Senate. During a two hour conference, both senators acknowledged the need for meaningful and enforceable civil rights legislation, but both expressed misgivings over aspects of the pending proposal and predicted additional difficulties in Congress before final enactment of the Civil Rights Act could become reality. For his part, Senator Dominick was aware of possible ramifications of the act for the Japanese American community and conveyed his personal regards to JACL members in Colorado, many of whom he had met recently at the Mountain-Plains JACL Convention in Denver. Although the spirit of the law must have heartened those in the Japanese American community who had felt the sting of exclusion, there is no indication that BJAA as a group ever took an official, public stand on the proposed legislation. Political involvement was avoided by the Brighton group, though practiced freely by individual members. The Civil Rights Act of 1964 became law in July. It barred racial segregation in public schools, at the workplace, and in the voting booth. It would be one of the lasting legal legacies of Lyndon Johnson's presidency.

Mike Tashiro frequently reminded BJAA members of the legacy that he felt the association was building locally. "I would like to stress that there is an important need for this Japanese American Association of ours in this community," he said. "Principally, [to] participate in Brighton community activities and projects," including the hospital and a new city swimming pool. No less important, he added, were the organization's youth baseball activities and its judo club. Unlike earlier city-sponsored baseball leagues that had barred JA kids from joining, the BJAA's teams were open to all kids in town, "for the general welfare of everyone."

Tim Matsuno, who was BJAA president for three years in the 1970s, traced his participation in the association as an adult to the three association sports he had enjoyed as a boy: baseball, judo, and bowling. His father, John Matsuno, was often called on to sing at association functions when the situation warranted, and his mother, Mary, was a local seamstress and active in the BNWC. Matsuno himself started playing BJAA baseball when he was about ten years old, in the late 1950s. His dad managed the team and Bill Chikuma coached. Matsuno remembered that before each season he and his teammates were driven to Gart Brothers, a sports store in Denver, to pick out equipment and uniforms. As kids, they took the trips for granted. "Honestly," he admitted, "when we were kids we just took advantage of everything that was going on. We played baseball and got to eat, and that was about the size of it. We didn't know where all the money was coming from." Toby Chikuma, Ray Imatani, Bob Sakaguchi, and Eddie Tashiro were among his teammates. Matsuno recalled that baseball games were called by Duke White. White was a licensed umpire and became a mentor to the players, a role he had filled since the 1930s when he worked with the Brighton Young Men's Association teams. He was possibly the only African American living in town for much of that time. White's name remains part of Brighton's sports history, on permanent display at the baseball facility behind BHS, now officially Duke White Field.

Judo classes, like this one in 1950, were offered by the BJAA to all kids in the Brighton area.

This BJAA-sponsored baseball team played during the summer of 1966.

This team enjoyed baseball in the summer of 1969.

Tim Matsuno and his teammates played against teams from Greeley and other Northern Colorado towns, on a field that would later become Brighton's BJAA Park. For yearly Labor Day tournaments, the BJAA baseball program hosted teams from as far away as Salt Lake City and Ogden, Utah. Matsuno played the catcher's position, but after one tournament he mentioned that he really wanted to be a pitcher. He began throwing the ball, which caught coach Chikuma's attention. Coach picked up a bat but "he couldn't hit me," Matsuno said. The following summer, Chikuma moved him to the pitcher's mound. For Matsuno, the day remains a fond memory. He and friends such as Paul Sasa and Harvey Tashiro also signed up for judo classes started by Bill Okubo and Chuck Mizunaga, both senseis, certified judo masters, and by head instructor Bill Chikuma, who had mastered the sport during his high school years in Japan. In 1961, when the BJAA judo classes were initiated, Don Tanabe had explained the rationale for the new offering in the organization's monthly newsletter: "Judo is fast becoming a world-wide sport. More and more U.S. colleges are including judo as one of their physical education classes. Also, the 1964 Olympic Games to be held in Japan will have judo as a major sport." Boys from age eight were eligible to participate, Tanabe wrote. "Tell your neighbors!" he went on, "This class is open to our *hakujin* [non-Japanese] friends, too."

Though sports were an emphasis for the BJAA and BNWC, the arts were not overlooked. For years it sponsored an evening of music and dance called the Cherry Blossom Musicale. It featured throngs of kids, some dancing in kimonos and singing in

Japanese; most echoing the repertoire of tunes being practiced by every other student musician in every other small town across America. On a February night in 1959, the Musicale regaled the JA community with a variety show worthy of early television's Ed Sullivan. An ensemble called the JAA Band played the John Phillip Sousa march *Stars and Stripes Forever.* Sharon Masunaga and Karen Tazawa twirled to the *Colonel Bogey March* and *Muskrat Ramble,* recorded pieces that were staples of a baton twirling craze sweeping the country. Reed players Sharon Tani, Judy Sasaki, and Joan Sato collaborated on *Clarinet Polka,* definitely not a traditional Japanese tune. The program showcased vocal solos, piano duets, and the clarinet trio; not to mention dances: tap, ballet, Japanese, and hula. In all, the Musicale featured thirty-three numbers by fifty children under high school age. It was a night to swell the pride of any parent or grandparent who ever paid for private music lessons. And it brought the JA community together under one roof. The adults got in on the act too, quite literally. Jim and Sam Tochihara harmonized with Sam and Tosh Tashiro in a song titled *Hatoba Shigeru* arranged for quartet. Don Tanabe and Wesley Koyano were two of the members who chaired the Musicales in different years. Mary Sakata served as dance director, and Sumi Koyano, a talented musician herself, was music director and "the force behind the talent shows."

The BNWC began making another important contribution to the JA community as many of the early members' kids approached high school graduation. The women established a college scholarship program during the presidency of Sumie Imatani, in 1962. Imatani had graduated from the University of Colorado with a degree in nursing and was well known for her beautiful quilts. The first recipient of the annual scholarship was Paul Sasa. The program continued for many years on a competitive basis. Over time, however, the number of applicants declined. One theory for the decline was that members knew each other's kids so well that they could foresee the obvious winners and chose not to apply on behalf of their own. In light of this trend, BNWC members decided to give a cash grant to every eligible graduate. Eligibility is now based on just two conditions: a recipient must have helped with the Chow Mein Dinners and his or her parents must be members of the BJAA.

By the end of the turbulent decade of the 1960s, there had been a major change in the local community's perceptions of the Japanese Americans among them. Paul Okada made the following comment about his two terms as BJAA president in 1967 and 1968: "I do know the BJAA and the Japanese community were very well accepted in Brighton and the surrounding areas because of the donations to various charities and organizations started by previous cabinet members and continued by mine." A good number of the group's original purposes had seemingly been accomplished. The good works would continue.

CHAPTER SIX:

Continuing The Mission

Linda Kline remembers a minor rite of passage experienced by most kids of BJAA and BNWC parents: working at the annual Chow Mein Dinner. For the first few years, she looked forward to serving tea; it was a step up from selling dinner tickets door to door. Soon, "volunteering" became more of an imposed task – a natural reaction for a young person – but Kline still remembers her early participation fondly. As social events, the dinners broadened her familiarity with the JA community. She had become involved in club-sponsored activities as early as age four, dancing in a kimono and traditional makeup with Vicki Sakata and Yoko Koyano. "It was a big thing for me," Kline said. During her childhood years, her brothers were involved in athletics: Bruce played basketball, and Ron competed in judo. Current BJAA president Diane Dible recalled similar childhood impressions. "The women of my mother's generation were good examples to their children by conducting club activities in such a businesslike manner and serving others," Dible said. But "they always had a lot of fun, too."

David Tashiro wistfully recalled his early participation with the group. "I have very fond memories of BJAA when I was little," he said. "There were no cell phones, no video games. It seems like we always did everything together," which was part of the attraction for him as a kid when ski trips to the mountains were his favorite activity. The group usually went to Winter Park, though on one special day they went to Vail. "We got up way before anyone should be getting up, got all our food ready, and hopped on the bus, two or three busses every time we went. The kids would all go, and the grandparents would all sit and visit and have our food ready after we had skied all day." As with all association activities, "There was always food." To emphasize the point, Tashiro said again, "Everybody went: grandparents, parents, kids." Tashiro came by his participation naturally. He is the son of early organization members Hitoshi and Joyce (Tokunaga) Tashiro. David was president for a short time in 1994 and continues to be active.

In 1970 when Emi Chikuma became BNWC president, the women's club had no money in its treasury. "A meeting was held by all the cabinet officers," she said, "and we decided to sell candy to have a little help for our expenses. We did well thanks to the cabinet and sold our entire quota." In the meantime, Mieko Mayeda and a few of the other members asked the men's association for help to finance their year. "We paid them back with thanks," remembered Chikuma. The post-dinner evaluation notes from the 1971 Chow Mein Dinner showed continued success for the event. Expectations had been for 1,800 patrons; 2,122 showed up. "Naturally," the note pointed out with some understatement, "there was some last minute running around." Also mentioned was Hazel Tani, who "still makes the best chow mein in the Rocky Mountain area."

In 1974, the women decided it was time to expand the slim cookbook they had published years earlier. Joanna Sakata volunteered to chair a committee to gather and organize recipes from the membership, not realizing how time consuming the process would become. Once a week for almost a year, she and seven others – Hazel Tani, Emi Chikuma, Yasuko Tochihara, Sumi Mizunaga, Carol Kishiyama, Faye Kanda, and Marta Matsuno – met weekly to prepare *Eastern Western Food*, 300 spiral-bound pages of recipes and cooking tips. As anyone who has ever watched programming on the Food Network knows, the best cooks prepare meals to taste, with a "pinch" of this spice and a "dash" of that one. Such were the methods of many of the club's older members who submitted their traditional recipes for the publication. To convert those traditional pinches and dashes into more standard measurements, committee members had to visit fragrant kitchens and peek over the shoulders of those cooks in action. Sampling was allowed, one hopes. "We made nuisances of ourselves," said Sumi Mizunaga, "checking and double checking recipes with the members." Art work for the book was done by Hylam Shimoda.

Initially, committee members pictured the cookbook as a means of preserving Japanese culinary customs for their children. At the time of its publication, Joanna Sakata said, "We find that as generations pass on, many wonderful and good things, including recipes, pass on." The cookbook was given a more international flare with the addition of recipes from other cultures as well, reflective of Brighton itself. "We hope that [this cookbook] will make us all aware that even though our physical features and cultural traits are different," the committee wrote on their dedication page, "our basic needs are the same." And, of course, *Eastern Western Food* would be a fundraising tool, which it continues to be today. The first printing of 1,000 copies sold out within ten days. A second printing of 1,200 was quickly ordered. To date, the BNWC cookbook has sold almost 8,000 copies.

Within the book's covers are recipes from soup to nuts, literally. Recipes range from simple to fancy; from traditional to contemporary. Some, like that for miso soup, might be difficult to find elsewhere. Making chow mein for one hundred? Get the recipe from the pros. How to cook rice? Properly, of course, and the directions are there. So are recipes for beef teriyaki, wontons, *buta no kushi sashi*, a pork dish, and *yose-nabe*, a casserole. For the latter, you'll need shrimp, chicken, bamboo shoots, China peas, mushrooms, carrots, and beef stock, and, of course, soy sauce. Have a taste for an international meal tonight? Try Greek *pastitsio*, Italian meatballs, Mexican chicken, or German cabbage bread.

The Nisei Women's Club often met for lunch at the Terrace Inn in Brighton. Attending one meeting in 1977 were (left to right) Yoskiko Nakata, Helen Okada, Hazel Tani and Haruko Sasa.

Also in attendance at the 1977 BNWC meeting were (left to right) Helen Fukaye, Doris Nakata, Mary Chikuma and Mary Tokunaga.

For the men of the BJAA, upkeep on the six-acre baseball field at Twelfth and Longs Peak proved to be quite a thorny issue. Dr. John Chikuma, president in 1966, answered many phone calls from neighborhood residents about "the ground stickers, weeds, and bull head that were growing there." Chikuma also heard angry accounts of swirling "dust storms." Another member reported "complaints, complaints, complaints." Then in early 1968 the idea to lease the land to the city began to circulate. President Paul Okada wrote a letter urging members to attend a general meeting to determine the future of the field. Okada reminded them that the primary reason the organization had purchased the land was to provide a ball field for the membership's children but acknowledged that maintenance had always been a problem. The organization had wanted to make improvements proposed by the city but was hindered by insufficient funds and manpower. "This seems to be a good opportunity to provide an ideal ball field for the kids," Okada wrote, "and at the same time get rid of a big maintenance headache." What the membership might want to do with the land in the future would determine the decision. In the democratic spirit of BJAA, Okada concluded his letter with an exhortation: "This is your property, so please come and join in the discussion to help make a decision."

Deliberations with the Brighton City Council began in February for the long-term lease – twenty-five years at one dollar per year, basically a donation – with development of the lot by the city as a combination public park and ball field. Initial plans included an underground sprinkler system, sod, picnic tables, and grills. The plan was deemed "a significant step toward total community conservation and use of available open space land." Members of the JA community were already active in the beautification of Brighton. Jim Kiyota of Brighton Florist and Nursery, for example, donated thousands of flowers each spring for planting in the city's parks. Funding for the development of the new park was expected to come from a combination of local donations and federal grants. That funding, evidently, did not materialize. Even though BJAA president Paul Okada signed a lease with Brighton mayor Ken Mitchell, the leasing process was repeated in 1971 by president Ken Mizunaga. In 1973, the BJAA, under president Tim Matsuno, donated the lot outright to the city, which at some point invested $50,000 for improvements and finally dedicated the park in October of 1976, eight years after the initial deliberations. The Brighton Japanese American Association Park included a baseball diamond, of course, and tennis courts and a picnic area. A Japanese *tori* gate directed visitor to the park's entrance. Front and center, before a crowd of approximately one hundred in attendance at a dedication ceremony, were BJAA president Roy Mayeda and BNWC president June Tagawa. Three Japanese folk dances were performed by a troupe consisting of Emi and Josephine Chikuma, Betty Jo Doi, Carol Kishiyama, Sumi Mizunaga, Deko Shibao, Gale Tagawa, and Yasuko Tochihara. The Brighton High jazz band also performed, prompting the observation that the ceremony was "an interesting blend of Japanese and American cultures."

BJAA Park may have been eight years in the making, but for the leadership of both organizations there were plenty of other issues discussed and activities initiated during the 1970s. Members assisted with new landscaping in front of the former Adams County Administration Building on Fourth Avenue, which they did again in 1993. For the first time, the men's and women's organizations entered a float in the Adams County Fair Parade. The float, and the kimonoed dancers who followed it, caught the community's attention, and that of parade judges who named the joint venture the event's grand prize winner for 1976, the year of the U.S. Bicentennial. The float builders repeated their win the following summer.

BJAA and BNWC members entered a Japanese-themed float in the Adams County Fair Parade in 1976. Members involved in construction included (left to right) Sam Tashiro, Chuck Shibao, Tom Shibao, Ken Mizunaga and Roy Mayeda.

Women of the BNWC danced along the Adams County Fair route in 1977.

Also that year, Deko Shibao began recruiting BNWC volunteers for scheduled visits at the Brighton Care Center, where many of the older Issei were spending their final years. Fudge Tashiro, one of the first to volunteer for the service project, said, "We would visit them, take food, mostly Japanese food, or craft items. Sometimes we would put on programs for them, such as Japanese singing and getting the younger ones to perform Japanese *odori*," traditional dances. The monthly visits initiated by Shibao continued well into the 1990s. She is praised as a member who was instrumental in the club's continued welfare.

Politics dominated the collective American mind in the 1970s. The divisive war in Vietnam was winding down under Richard Nixon's administration, but revelations of improprieties during his reelection were coming to light, which would lead to his resignation from office in 1974. Politics was certainly on the mind of Tim Matsuno, three-term BJAA president beginning in 1973. He advocated that the association begin expressing opinions on ballot issues and supporting local candidates, to exert some political muscle in Adams County. It was a somewhat radical idea, Matsuno admitted. Politics had been intentionally avoided by the association since its founding.

From Japanese Americans across the country there were an increasing number of demands that some form of reparation – at very least a formal apology – be given by the federal government to the 120,000 Issei and Nisei who had been displaced or imprisoned in 1942. Foremost among those making the case for reparation was Min Yasui. Tim Matsuno, on behalf of BJAA, took part in exploratory discussions of the topic of reparations with Yasui and other JACL members in Denver. Matsuno's involvement sent him home feeling a sense of discomfort with the traditional, neutral stance assumed by the BJAA toward the political arena. "I was uncomfortable with the way that BJAA was going, and I wanted it to get involved in more than just civic stuff," Matsuno recalled. "We ought to pick people that we want to see in the city council and the school board. We ought to flex our muscles a little bit and get way more active politically," possibly even entering a BJAA-designated candidate for a local office. Within the leadership, more moderate voices prevailed. "It didn't take but one [board] meeting to have me put back in my place," Matsuno said, admitting that at the time he was angered by the group's rebuff. In his words, "My fellow board members said, Look, we're not here to take over a town. We're here to fit into a town. We worked our whole lives after the war to be accepted by the community. If we [feel we] have to move people in a direction, we can move them by talking to them [as individuals], because they're our friends," as Seiji Horiuchi had when running for the Colorado legislature. Taking the association into politics, the argument ran, could create a backlash against all that the membership had accomplished to date. Under Tim Matsuno's leadership and beyond, the BJAA, as well as the BNWC, avoided politics, continuing to dedicate itself to fostering good community relations through dedicated community service.

"At the time I didn't see the wisdom in that position," Matsuno said recently, "but today I really do. If a group takes a stand politically, all the members of the group are perceived to share that stand," an assumption sure to misrepresent some or all in any organization like the BJAA. Matsuno also saw a similar line of thinking in the internal workings of the president's cabinet. "I don't remember ever taking a vote and saying, Okay, if the majority says this, that's what we're going to do," he said of his three years in office. "If we didn't have consensus, I don't think we [took action]." Discussion continues among the leadership until consensus is reached. "The minority opinion really matters in JAA and BNWC. The group moves as a group. That is part of the strength of the group. I didn't see it at first as an outsider."

Tim Matsuno, BJAA president in 1973 and 1974.

In 1980, when Jeanette Mayeda was elected president of BNWC, the hospital was adding on to its facility and needed help. "The one thing I remember," she wrote, "is having an election to donate to the Brighton hospital. This has been so long ago, but we voted to add the furniture to one room, and when the voting was finished it passed to equip one room," a seemingly small but nevertheless significant contribution. Social activities continued, too, during her term. "We all enjoyed ourselves on the ski trip and our picnic held at Dillon Reservoir," she wrote.

In 1982, Bob Sakaguchi became one of the first Sansei to serve as president of BJAA. His Brighton roots go back to his pioneering grandparents, Katsubei and Hisano Sakaguchi. At a recent informal gathering of current organization members, Sakaguchi acknowledged the "vision and tenacity" of the founders in conceiving the two organizations. "The contributions that both clubs have made over the years to the community at large," he added, "go beyond commendations and mere accolades. They are responsible for the respect and admiration of all Americans of Japanese ancestry in Brighton, the state of Colorado, and even the nation." And most importantly, he said, "They have provided a set of values, standards, and a sense of caring for our families and our communities." By Sakaguchi's term as president, the Chow Mein Dinner was being served at the present Adams County Fairgrounds, but that year the dining area was moved from a small meeting room to the much larger rotunda area, its present location. The number of diners grew to 2,900 in 1982 – 800 more than a decade earlier.

One key to the organization's success for sixty-plus years has been the process it employs in generating candidates for leadership positions. It's a twofold model: part passing on of traditions, part training in civic leadership. Yet frankly, a third element is also put into play: applying the traditional Japanese sense of obligation directly to the consciences of potential board members. The annual slate of candidates is filled in a "very democratic method," asserted long-time officer Bob Sakata. "The board votes and puts names on the ballot." Does the board always solicit consent from candidates before posting their names on the ballot? Sakata considered the question carefully, for more than a few seconds, and then smiled, admitting, "Sometimes we don't." Minoru Tagawa offered additional insight to the process: "If you don't attend the nominating meeting, your name goes on the ballot…and they don't always tell you when the meeting is." Tagawa himself was elected vice president three years in a row before serving five terms as president, from 2006 through 2010. Tagawa's father, Albert, and his uncles Ken and Dave all served on the board from time to time.

Ron Ida told a similar story of being finessed into leadership roles. A BHS student officer for the class of 1961, Ida spent a four-year stint in the military after high school before finishing degree work at the University of Colorado, Boulder, then returned to Brighton and worked for his dad in the family produce business in Denver. He joined BJAA in the mid-1970s and was asked by Sam Tashiro to serve on his committee, which was in charge of buying groceries for the dinners. "That was the start of it," Ida laughed. "Sam Tashiro had an ulterior motive. He was grooming me to take over the committee. And I fell for it," Ida laughed again. "By 1980, I was doing all the buying for the dinners." It was a role in which he clearly excelled. He has been the volunteer purchasing agent for the dinner for thirty years.

"Sam Tashiro liked the idea of turning the reigns over to the younger guys," Ida said. "So that's why I got 'roped' into [an office] so early." Tashiro's approach to leadership was deceptively simple – and familiar. Tashiro's advice, according to Ida, was "Just do it!" Speaking of his early experience with the organization's unofficial leadership training program, Ida said, "It really helped me. Sam was such an outgoing and nice guy that he was able to get along with a lot of people. He never burned bridges or got mad at people. He was always upbeat. So I tried to be the same way." Ida was elected vice president in 1981 and reelected the next year. "And then the other JAA officers tricked me," he said, laughing yet again. "They said, You know the vice president automatically becomes president." And that's how Ron Ida came to serve as president in 1983 and 1984. "[The other officers] and I became really good friends," he added. "I used to go fishing with Sam a lot. If it wasn't for the club, I probably wouldn't have gotten to know the older generation that well."

Ron Ida and the other, younger officers took the leadership football and ran with it. During his terms as vice president and president, the club didn't have much money to work with, a perennial problem. "We lived from year to year when it came to our donations and civic activities," he said. "About the time that I was VP was when they started to let the younger generation take over." Despite the efforts of officers like Sam Tashiro, some Nisei found it hard to hand off responsibilities to their juniors, having grown used to handling things themselves. "My friend Bob Sakaguchi was president before

I was, and we decided we needed to do something [about the club's financial situation]. We started really pushing the Chow Mein Dinner as a fundraiser because we needed the operating funds." Sakaguchi, Ida, and Dave Tagawa, three presidents in a row, decided to bump up the fundraising. "We just decided that the club needed to go in a different direction," Ida said, "and make some real money for some real civic activity."

Bob Sakaguchi, BJAA president in 1982.

Ron Ida, BJAA president in 1983 and 1984.

Dave Tagawa, BJAA president in 1985 and 1986.

Nationwide, by the early 1980s, talk of reparations could no longer be ignored. Former internees, such as Frank Torizawa of Denver, were insisting on an apology from the U.S. government for the internments it had forced on them in 1942. Torizawa and his wife had been held for ten months, housed in a horse stall at California's Santa Anita Race Track, which had been hurriedly converted into an "assembly center." In 1944, they were transferred to an internment center called Camp Amache, near the small town of Granada in southeast Colorado. After the war, the Torizawas moved to Denver, where Frank opened a fish market: The Granada. During the war, Torizawa and others in his situation had accepted internment as *shikata ga nai*, a thing which cannot be helped. Forty years later, he felt that an official government apology was in order. Torizawa was quoted as saying, "[Government officials] knew they were wrong. They must admit they were wrong." BJAA's Tim Matsuno remembered the same theme

being expressed: "Whenever we met with JACL in Denver...
all they wanted from the United States was an apology. Just
say you were wrong."

The JACL formed a committee, including Min Yasui, that
made a formal proposal to Congress regarding reparations.
But not everyone in the Japanese American community agreed
with the approach being taken. "I pleaded with the [BJAA
and JACL] leadership at that time not to involve money," said
Bob Sakata, a former internee himself. "Don't involve money.
That would cheapen what we went through. Let's pass a bill in
Congress that makes them publish an apology in every damn
newspaper in America. That will do better." In 1980, Congress
formed an investigative group with a typically lengthy bu-
reaucratic name: the Presidential Commission on Wartime
Relocation and Internment of Civilians. It held many days of
hearings in Washington. Former U.S. Senator S. I. Hayakawa
of California shared Sakata's passion against monetary pay-
ments. The concept of reparations was offensive to the pride of
older Japanese Americans, he contended. Referring to military
units such as the 442nd RCT, he said that reparations were "to-
tally unnecessary in view of the fact that Japanese Americans
re-established their loyalty and their honor in blood, damn
it, in blood." Nevertheless, a Chicago-based group called the
National Council for Japanese American Redress did file a
class action lawsuit against the federal government, seeking financial compensation for the surviving victims of internment
and asking the court to declare that the U.S. had violated their
constitutional, statutory, and civil rights

During this time, crucial documents were obtained from U.S. government agencies under the Freedom of Information Act by Peter H. Irons, a lawyer and professor of political science at the University of California-San Diego. The documents showed that at the time of Min Yasui's appeal to the Supreme Court, officials of the War Department had persuaded the Justice Department to withhold a key footnote questioning its justification for Japanese internment and other wartime restrictions, such as the curfew that Yasui had defied in Portland. Consequently, Yasui and two other defendants filed papers in three federal courts contending that their civil rights had been violated. The newly discovered documents clearly showed that no Japanese Americans had engaged in acts of espionage after Pearl Harbor, as the War Department had contended. The case against Yasui, which justified his imprisonment because of military necessity, no longer had validity. His criminal conviction was overturned by the federal court in 1986. Some in the Brighton community had never been comfortable with the political activism of individuals like Min Yasui. They felt that such activism was "making waves" and would further alienate Japanese Americans from the White population.

By 1983, the presidential commission in Washington had drawn together its findings and made a definitive conclusion, published in a document titled *Personal Justice Denied*. The internment of Japanese Americans in 1942 was not justified, it said. In the opinion of the commission, the reasons behind internment were "race prejudice, war hysteria, and a failure of political leadership," not military threat. Commission members did indeed recommend a national apology, but they also called for a lump-sum payment of $20,000 to each of some sixty thousand remaining survivors of the internment camps. The recommended payments were estimated to cost a total $1.5 billion.

It took Congress until August of 1988 to pass legislation acting on the recommendations of the commission. The Civil Liberties Act of 1988 provided a presidential apology and the symbolic payment of $20,000 to each internee, evacuee, or other person of Japanese ancestry who lost liberty or property because of discriminatory action by the federal government during World War II. It was signed into law by President Ronald Reagan. Min Yasui, activist and friend of the BJAA, never saw the result of his participation in the redress movement. Yasui died at age seventy in 1986. "We have lost a good friend," eulogized Congressman Norman Mineta of California, "and this country has lost a leader in the struggle for equal justice under law."

An official letter of apology was sent to surviving Issei and Nisei internees in 1990, some fifty years after their imprisonment. Signed by President George H.W. Bush, the short letter said in part:

> A monetary sum and words alone cannot restore lost years or erase painful memories; neither can they fully convey our Nation's resolve to rectify injustice and to uphold the rights of individuals. We can never fully right the wrongs of the past. But we can take a clear stand for justice and recognize that serious injustices were done to Japanese Americans during World War II.

A decade later the Justice Departments' Office of Redress Administration closed its doors, having paid out more than $1.6 billion to more than eighty-two thousand individuals of Japanese ancestry. "This was a tragic chapter in the history of our nation," said Attorney General Janet Reno in 1999. "The U.S. Government recognized the injustice of its actions during the war and provided a presidential apology and compensation. It was a time when we took away the liberty of an entire community of Americans."

Sometime in 1988, the BJAA and the BNWC caught up with national trends in association memberships and equality of the sexes. BNWC president Emi Chikuma approached BJAA president Bob Sakata about merging their two organizations. The aims of the two organizations were almost identical, and their activities were often done in tandem. In 1953, Rose Tanabe had served as the sixth president of the women's group. In 1989, she was again selected for that office, the final official leader of the Brighton Nisei Women's Club. The club had forty-nine members at the time, with an average age of about seventy. "I would like to have us continue," she said somewhat reluctantly. Member Mary Shibao agreed: "I feel it's a shame if we lose everything that our parents have brought to us and our heritage." The combined organization set its sights on being more family-oriented. "This way," said Bob Sakata, "the whole family – the husband, the wife, and the children – can participate." The BJAA also intended to develop a youth leadership training program. Bob Sakaguchi explained further: "We need to bring the younger generation to infuse their ideas and philosophy." By 1991, the merger was official. The 150 members of the men's association joined the fifty members of the women's club in electing the first "co-ed" cabinet of a revitalized BJAA.

Other changes were evolving, too. Dr. Bob Larson became the first hakujin to join the organization, in the early 1980s. BJAA bylaws were changed to accommodate his membership. His wife, Becky, formerly Becky Takahashi, had been BNWC president in 1984. Others followed the open membership trend. Current member Richard Brookman started dating Sandy Tashiro when they were both in seventh grade. "From the moment I stepped into the Japanese community, I never felt like an outsider," Brookman said. "The group has always welcomed outsiders." Despite the long hair and beard he sported during high school and the "gnarly hotrod" he drove, Brookman said, "I always felt part of Sam Tashiro's family." Richard, with wife Sandy in agreement, said "Our kids always say 'I'm not going to marry anyone Japanese because we're all related.' We're not really all related, but we call many club members Auntie or Uncle. And they're always there for us."

Mae Murata, the BNWC's last secretary, wrote in her year-end report – her "last official duty" as secretary of the women's club – "It is my hope that each one of us will evaluate ourselves and continue to grow and pass on the sense of dignity, integrity, and the pride of our culture." She added a quote from American novelist Nathaniel Hawthorne: "Every individual has a place to fill in the world and is important in some respect, whether he chooses to be so or not."

Past presidents of the BNWC gathered in 1989, the final year of the club's existence before merging with the BJAA. Top row (left to right): June Tagawa, Masaye Doi, Jane Tashiro, Mary Ida, Helen Fukaye, Yasuko Tashiro, Jan Mayeda, Helen Kurachi Sasaki, Haruko Sasa, Fuzzy Hisamoto, Rose Tanabe and Karen Tagawa. Bottom row (left to right): Fudge Tashiro, Emi Chikuma, Mary Tokunaga, Katherine Sakaguchi, Sumie Imatani, Helen Okada, Joanna Sakata, Josephine Fukaye, Misaye Uno and Sumiko Mizunaga.

CHAPTER SEVEN:

Chow Mein

Describing the annual BJAA Chow Mein Dinner without slipping into cliché poses a challenge not unlike mounting the extravaganza itself. From a distance, if one squints a bit, that white dome at the fairgrounds could be mistaken for a huge bee hive. Inside, a swarm of diners buzzes with conversation, much of it among friends who seem not to have spoken since the previous year's dinner. Tea servers dart through a honeycomb labyrinth of tables. And central to this swarm of activity is the production and delivery of nourishment. The analogy is far from perfect. No queen commands attention at the center of this hive. And the worker bees are smiling and accommodating, not at all like mindless drones, though they fulfill their pre-ordained duties with a similar precision and grace.

Then again, with its cast of hundreds working under the tent-like dome, the BJAA dinner also resembles a traveling circus that has brought its exotic sights and sounds and aromas to town on yet another spring afternoon. Behind the scenes, prep rooms hum with urgency and the occasional good-natured heckling. Shrimp wranglers tame their charges in cages bubbling with dangerously hot oil. Under the big top, crowds circle the center ring in anticipation of the main event. No popcorn or cotton candy is hawked, but tables filled with homemade confections are just as tempting. There are no heart stopping leaps from a high trapeze and no one is shot from a cannon, but preparing and serving meals to upwards of 3,000 diners in one afternoon certainly involves genuine cooperative daring.

How does it all come together? The shrimp order may be made up to a year in advance, to lock in the best price, but "normally around October or November when the price is low," said chief buyer Ron Ida. After the oil spill in the Gulf of Mexico in 2010, shrimp prices became consistently higher than they had been. The vegetables are purchased fresh from California or Mexico through wholesale houses; since the dinner is held in the spring, local crops are not yet available. Ida buys "dry goods" from Costco and other wholesale outlets. "Ketchup is a big thing," he said with a smile. "There aren't many places where you can buy a one-and-a-half-gallon container of ketchup. So whenever Costco gets it in and it's cheap, I buy it. It's kind of funny, but I'm always on the lookout."

Ron Ida also gave some historical perspective on how the preparation and execution of the dinners have been streamlined. "At first it was pretty hard because we had to do everything by hand. We had to clean all the vegetables. We had to cook everything from scratch. It was four days of hard work." Ida observed other organizations whose main fund raisers were food bazaars or dinners. "They started going downhill because it was hard to get volunteers." Noting that some BJAA volunteers were getting disenchanted and even ending their participation, the leadership identified trouble spots in its own operation. "We found out that to keep the dinners successful, we had to keep the volunteers happy." That meant lessening the work load and making the time commitment fair for everybody. "Every year we'd figure out ways to make it easier and easier," Ida said. For example, the association is now able to buy most of the needed vegetables pre-cut and pre-prepared, such as chopped celery and shredded coleslaw.

"We used to ask volunteers to start at 6 A.M. on the Sunday morning of the dinner," Ida noted, "and we wouldn't finish until nine or ten that night, largely due to the amount of post-dinner clean-up needing to be done. And everyone, regardless of their role, was asked to stay for those clean-up sessions. "We identified that as the number one thing that people hated to do." Volunteers worked all day and still had to stay to help clean up the facility. "So we formed a separate clean-up crew that came in at the end of the dinner so that everyone else could go home at three o'clock. Everyone loved that change." He added, "Now we pretty much have the dinner down to a science."

"There are a lot of fundraising activities that have gone by the wayside and a lot of clubs that aren't in existence anymore," Ida said. "But ours keeps thriving. And we're not a national organization, just a small, local group." One secret to success is that extended families within the organization have adopted specific committees as their own. This enables family members to put some good old-fashioned parental and familial pressure on each other to staff their committee with "volunteers" and get the work done. And, of course, business contributions have sustained the dinners as well. Pacific Mercantile in Denver donates thousands of dollars to the dinner, 500 pounds of rice per year and the use of a truck to haul supplies back and forth to the fair grounds. The Simpson United Methodist Church in Arvada loans eighteen large rice cookers for use each year. Sakata Farms recently donated an eighteen-wheel rig that serves as a storage unit for all supplies and cooking gear between dinners. Tagawa Greenhouses donates the use of a refrigerated truck for the dinner weekend as well.

Volunteers still do prep work on the dinner weekend. One committee butterflies shrimp on Friday evening. Others pack plastic utensils and napkins for take-out orders and prepare garnishes for the chow mein on Saturday, which is a much more casual session than previously when bulk celery, onions, and cabbage had to be sliced and bagged. On the day of the big event, breakfast is served for the volunteers at 6 A.M., and the doors open for lunch at eleven.

"Today the BJAA is getting really active," observed Ron Ida. "I think that's because of the younger generation." Ida feels that the association has been able to attract younger members better than other ethnic or service organizations. Considering the third, fourth, and fifth generations of Japanese Americans in the area, "we could probably gather two hundred volunteers [for a cause] if we had to." And not all volunteers are association members. BJAA has a bountiful list of friends and relatives who also sign up repeatedly for work shifts. Speaking for the group, Ida expressed sentiments that an outsider unfamiliar with the spirit and purpose behind the dinners might find odd. "We've been pretty fortunate over the past few years," he said. But not fortunate because of the profits the club has been able to make. "Fortunate" because of the funds they've been able to give away. "We've been able to make some fairly decent contributions." That comment reflects a humility that might be incomprehensible to an outsider. Over the history of the BJAA, the contributions to local and national charities have reached half a million dollars. "Fairly decent," indeed.

The course of the Chow Mein Dinner took an ironic turn after the 1998 dinner drew a record-breaking turnout: three thousand meals served. The following year, for the first time, members asked that a vote of the entire organization be taken to determine the fate of future dinners. Ballots were mailed to all members, asking whether a dinner should be held or not in spring 1999. By a narrow margin, they said it should not. The reasoning of those opposed seemed to be straightforward: preparations for the dinner had become too exhausting. The cabinet and many members were disappointed in the vote. Whatever reasons members may have had about the fate of the 1999 dinner, a hiatus of one year seemed to be needed to revitalize participants. The following year a similar vote to re-instate the dinner garnered seventy-three votes in favor and only forty-three against. In his first term as president, Kirk Horiuchi oversaw the restarting of the fundraising dinners. "Many members believed that they just needed the one-year break to refocus and reenergize," he said. The charitable giving, however, continued. In March, $500 donations were designated for each of five local service providers: Almost

Home, the Brighton Senior Center, the Japanese American Community Graduation Program, Dollars for Scholars, and Meals on Wheels. Grants to members' high school graduates also continued.

During four terms as president, Kirk Horiuchi spent time reflecting on the basic role of the organization and discussing his thoughts with other members. As he was aware, part of the association's initial mission was to provide a setting for socialization among the Brighton Nisei still being excluded from community activities in the wake of World War II. But in the fifty-year progression of the BJAA, exclusion had been turned to acceptance. In addition, only eighty-eight of 169 members at the time were residents of the immediate Brighton area. Almost half of the membership lived in the greater Denver area. The long-term Brighton family names were still prominent on the roster, though, with Horiuchi, Okada, Tashiro, Chikuma, Sasa, and Tagawa appearing most often. Yet, Horiuchi felt a need to redirect the mission statement for the organization. He also felt a need to attract more members from the younger generations. "Most of those who come to the meetings are of my father's generation," Horiuchi wrote of his four terms in the cabinet. "Fewer and fewer Sansei and *Yonsei* (fourth generation Japanese Americans) show up for meetings, events, and functions." He then asked rhetorically, "Are we as a generation too busy for these kinds of things?" Horiuchi had himself been involved with the organization since childhood, about forty years at that time, and had served in the cabinet for over fifteen. In 2000, he oversaw the celebration of the BJAA's fiftieth anniversary celebration.

Kirk Horiuchi, BJAA president from 1999 through 2002, presided over the fiftieth anniversary activities of the association.

That landmark celebration culminated with a fall gala at Denver's historic Brown Palace Hotel. Among the 190 in attendance were the Japanese Consul General, Koichiro Seki; newspaper man Bill Hosokawa; and the BJAA's first president, George Masunaga. In comments before the assembled members and guests, Hosokawa alluded to the terrorist attacks that had rocked the world just a month prior to the gala and were still painfully fresh in the minds of his listeners. For its shocking suddenness, September 11 was to be a new generation's December 7. "We meet tonight in troubled times," Hosokawa began, "to celebrate what is noble, what is generous, what is laudable in the human spirit. It is an occasion to review the meaning of compassion and understanding at a time when, throughout much of the world, there is little but hate and anger and fear...It is reassuring to know that in this small corner of the world, people of different ethnic backgrounds and different faiths can join together in the common goal of making their community a better place for all." He concluded by congratulating the members of the BJAA for their fifty years of public service "in the noblest American tradition."

George Masunaga made a few comments, referring to the organization's predecessor, the Nihonjin Kai, and BJAA honorary members John T. Horie and Min Yasui. He also mentioned that in the early years the organization was cash poor. "We couldn't support civic duties, so for one project, we went to thin sugar beets. I think we were paid about $2.00 an acre." Kirk Horiuchi wrote, "After listening to Bill Hosokawa, George Masunaga and Bob Sakata, I have a renewed respect for what the Nisei have endured to create and maintain this organization. It is up to us Sansei and Yonsei to find a cause for the organization that we can embrace with the same dedication."

Due to the volunteer spirit of its individual members, the BJAA was no longer cash poor. In 2001, they voted to donate $5,000 to the Brighton Police Department, helping it hire an artist to create a sixteen-by-forty-foot mural inside its new building. In 2003, when Stan Shibao became president, the membership voted to make the largest donation in its fifty-plus year history. "I remember in my first year as president," Shibao wrote. "The new Platte Valley Medical Center was just breaking ground in Brighton and the members decided to donate $15,000 over three years to get our new hospital off the ground. It turns out that our donation was the first non-profit community donation of its kind to the new medical center." Ties to Japan, of course, remain strong for members. The devastating tsunami that hit the northern coast of that country in 2011 prompted calls for help. The BJAA designated $5,000 from its coffers for relief efforts in Japan. The funds were channeled through the Japanese American Society of Colorado, a cultural and business link between the state and the country of Japan, and directly to the Consulate General of Japan at Denver, thus avoiding administrative costs that would have subtracted from the gift. The donation was part of a statewide effort totaling $128,000.

Cooking for the local Special Olympics in 2012 were (left to right) Ron Matsushima, Dick Chikuma, Shelley Tashiro, Stuart Tashiro and Josh Tashiro.

One chapter of the Japanese American story in Brighton came to a conclusion in the fall of 2005 when the Buddhist Temple there closed its doors. The temple's membership had declined to just twenty followers of the teachings of Buddha. Most of them were in their seventies and eighties, and they could no longer afford to maintain the building, site of so many BJAA social events and organizational meetings during its sixty-five years. As the arc of history would have it, the remaining members planned to worship together monthly in their homes, as members had when they initiated services in 1922. "I'm grateful for the time we had to worship in this building," said Mary Shibao, a long-time member, "but I'm glad that doors have been opened to us to worship in the homes."

Diane Dible set another first for the organization when she became president in 2011, the first woman elected to the position. Women had filled forty-one terms as president of the BNWC, of course, but Dible was the first to serve in that role for the combined association. The 2012 list of cabinet officers reflected additional diversity. Longtime member Ron Ida continued in the role of finance director, but Richard Brookman was elected vice president, and his college-age daughter, Nicole, filled the program chair. Nicole Brookman comes by her involvement naturally. Her grandfather, Sam Tashiro, had given countless hours to the association in its early decades. "My grandparents passed away when I was young," Brookman said, "so I didn't really know them, but since I have been part of the committee, I hear stories from other members about both of them and feel honored to be part of such a wonderful family whom so many people love and respect." Other younger members also showed signs of enthusiasm for membership and future involvement. Lindsay Auker noted the significance of the association in her family's history. "For my grandparents," she said, "the BJAA was a safe haven, a place where they could find acceptance and embrace the traditions and culture they had left behind in Japan." She acknowledged the role the BJAA has already played in her life as a "learning community" where those traditions are being preserved and passed on to her generation. It has also helped her create lifelong friendships and provided her with "the opportunity to get involved with the community while showing my pride in my Japanese heritage."

Diane Dible was first elected BJAA president in 2011.

Naomi Tashiro reflected on the progression of Japanese American families in Colorado's past, including her own. "As you grow up," she said, "you don't think about the little details of family history, how we integrated into society, and how we got to where we are. We just take it for granted." As an adult, Tashiro is fully engaged in her family history and in the extended family that is the Brighton Japanese American Association. As is member Dennis Kitayama. Although Kitayama grew up in California surrounded by other Japanese Americans, only later in life did he come to appreciate the path blazed by his elders. When he arrived in Colorado in the early 1980s, he was introduced to the BJAA, "indoctrinated," he said, through its bowling league. Now he serves as the civic chair in the cabinet. Before that he "used to come to meetings every once in a while, and helped out with chow mein dinners." Now he recognizes and appreciates the strong cohesiveness and sense of community he finds in the BJAA. "It's something you begin to appreciate as you age," Kitayama said. "We gravitate toward these things."

If the gravitational pull of community remains strong, this will not be the final chapter in the history of the Brighton Japanese American Association. The ongoing journey of the association and its member families, which began over one hundred years ago, will likely be influenced in the future more by societal trends than by earthshattering events. Yet, the membership hopes that an appreciation of the visions and sacrifices of the ancestors will enrich lives in the future. Without the stamina, hard work, dedication, and *gaman* shown by the Issei and Nisei, the successes of the present would not have been possible. In turn, the hope is that the experiences of the parents, grandparents, and great grandparents will inspire younger Japanese Americans – and the larger communities they inhabit – for generations to come.

The influence of BJAA members has been worldwide. In 1994 Emperor Akihito and Empress Michiko of Japan paid a rare visit to the U.S. At Sakata Farms, Joanna Sakata (left) explained a display of American farm techniques to the royal couple.

Sources

Blegen, Daniel. *Bob Sakata: American Farmer*. Palmer Lake, Colorado: Filter Press, 2009.

Brighton Blade. February 2, 1908; November 6, 1975; August 11, 1976; October 1, 1976; February 9, 1983; October 19, 2005.

Brighton Nisei Women's Club. *Eastern Western Food*.

Brokaw, Tom. *The Greatest Generation*. New York: Random House, 1998.

Brookman, Richard and Sandy. Interview by author. Henderson, Colorado. November 15, 2011.

Chikuma Family History. 1999.

Chikuma, Emi. Interview by author. Brighton, Colorado. May 6, 2011.

—. Interview by author. Brighton, Colorado. May 19, 2011.

—. Interview by author. Brighton, Colorado. June 20, 2011.

—. Manuscript. No Date.

—. Speech to the Brighton Nisei Women's Club, 1998.

Denver Post. April 4, 1954; September 4, 1977; April 7. 1082; January 19. 1983; October 2, 2005.

Encyclopedia of American Immigration. Carl L. Bankston, ed. Pasadena: Salem Press, Inc., 2010.

Fukui, Bill. Interview by author. Henderson, Colorado. November 15, 2011.

George Yoshito Masunaga. Gordon Studebaker, April, 2011.

Horiuchi, Glen and Shirley. Interview by author. Brighton, Colorado. March 15, 2012.

Horiuchi, Ken. Letter to author. March 5, 2012.

Hosokawa, Bill. *Colorado's Japanese Americans: From 1886 to the Present*. Boulder: University Press of Colorado, 2005.

—. *Nisei: The Quiet Americans*. Niwot, Colorado: University Press of Colorado, 1992.

—. "Purple Heart Regiment," *Rocky Mountain Empire Magazine*. July 4, 1948.

Ida, Ron. Interview by author. Brighton, Colo. October 29, 2011.

Japanese American Citizens League Bulletin. (Denver) March, 1948; December, 1948; May, 1950; December, 1950; January, 1951; February, 1951; December, 1952.

Japanese American History: An A-to-Z Reference from 1868 to the Present. Brian Niiya, ed. New York: Facts on File, Inc., 1993.

Kitiyama, Dennis. Interview by author. Henderson, Colo. November 15, 2011.

Kline, Linda. Interview by author. Brighton, Colo. July 20, 2011.

Koshi, George M., Letter to Emi Chikuma, September 10, 1985.

Longmont Ledger. (Longmont, Colorado) November 26, 1909.

Manchester, William. *The Glory and the Dream: A Narrative History of America, 1932-1972, Vol. 1.* Boston: Little, Brown and Company, 1973.

Market Place. (Brighton, Colorado) May 25, 1976; September 1, 1976.

Masunaga, George. Recorded comments. April, 2010.

Matsuno, Tim and Marta. Interview by author. Henderson, Colo. November 15, 2011.

Mizunaga Family History. Vicky Mizunaga Namura. 2000.

Mountain Plains A.J.A. News. (Denver) February, 1964.

Murray, Glen. Telephone conversation with author. August 30, 2011.

Noguchi, Donna. Interview by author. Henderson, Colo. November 15, 2011.

Nakata, Frank Takeshi. 1981.

Okada, Helen. Letter to author. March, 2011.

Pacific Citizen. (Los Angeles) March 4, 1977.

Reporter. (Denver) February, 1951.

Rocky Mountain Jiho. (Denver) December 22, 1976; October 23, 1978; June 18, 1980; June 25, 1980; July 9, 1980; July 16, 1980; July 30, 1980; August 6, 1980; August 20, 1980; August 27, 1980; September 10, 1980; September 17, 1980; September 24, 1980; October 1, 1980; October 8, 1980; October 15, 1980; October 22, 1980; November 5, 1980; November 19, 1980; December 3, 1980; December 31, 1980; August 12, 1981; October 14, 1981; January 5, 1983; September 21, 1983; September 28, 1983; June 14, 1989.

Rocky Mountain News. (Denver) January 7, 1944; February 2, 1944; September 21, 1975; December 6, 1982; February 25, 1983; March 17, 1983; June 18, 1983; August 12, 1990.

Rose Tanabe. Kathryn Stewart. 2005.

Sakaguchi Family History. 2004.

Sakaguchi, Bob. Interview with author. Lafayette, Colo. May 17, 2011.

Sakaguchi, Goro. Interview with author. Brighton, Colo. August 27, 2011.

Sakata, Bob. Interview by Daryl Maeda. May 14, 2008. http://archive.densho.org/main.aspx.

Schrager, Adam. *The Principled Politician: The Ralph Carr Story.* Golden, Colorado: Fulcrum Publishing, 2008.

Tagawa, Minoru. Interview by author. Henderson, Colo. November 15, 2011.

Tashiro, David and Barb. Interview by author. Henderson, Colo. November 15, 2011.

Tashiro, Fujiyo. Interview by author. August 27, 2011.

Tashiro, Jane. 1981.

Tashiro, Naomi. Interview by author. August 27, 2011.

Tazawa, Rose. Transcript of telephone conversation with Joanna Sakata, 2011.

Wagner, Albin. *Adams County: Crossroads of the West, Volume II.* 1987.

Watada, Alley. Interview by Richard Potashin. May 15, 2008. http://archive.densho.org/main.aspx.

Yampa Leader. (Yampa, Colorado) April 4, 1908.

Yasui, Robert S. *The Yasui Family of Hood River, Oregon.* Self-published, 1987.

Index of Names

About the Author

Daniel Blegen is the author of two biographies for young readers: *Bob Sakata: American Farmer* and *Ken Salazar: Joy in the Journey* and is coauthor of *Bent's Fort: Crossroads of Cultures on the Santa Fe Trail*. Blegen is a poet and playwright and has written about the arts for local newspapers and national magazines. He has taught English, journalism, speech, and drama at the middle school, high school, and community college levels. Blegen also performs American folk music, including a program titled Hard Travelin': The Life and Songs of Woody Guthrie. He lives in Longmont, Colorado.